STAYING SAFE

FOREWORD BY CHARLES W. COLSON

STAYING SAFE

Prison Fellowship's Guide to Crime Prevention

BETH SPRING

ZondervanPublishingHouse
Grand Rapids, Michigan

A Division of HarperCollinsPublishers

Staying Safe: Prison Fellowship's Guide to Crime Prevention
Copyright © 1994 by Prison Fellowship Ministries

Requests for information should be addressed to:
Zondervan Publishing House
Grand Rapids, Michigan 49530

Library of Congress Cataloging-in-Publication Data

Staying safe : Prison Fellowship's guide to crime prevention /
Prison Fellowship Staff with Beth Spring.
     p.   cm.
ISBN 0-310-40681-1
1. Crime prevention—United States. I. Spring, Beth. II. Prison
Fellowship Staff.
HV9950.S733 1994
362.88–dc20   93-51061
                                                          CIP

Edited by Rachel L. Boers
Interior design by Kim Koning, Sherri L. Korhorn
Cover design by Larry Taylor Design
Cover photo by The Image Bank

Printed in the United States of America

94 95 96 97 98 /❖ DH / 10 9 8 7 6 5 4 3 2 1

Contents

Changing the System

Acknowledgments

The assistance of many individuals within and outside Prison Fellowship made this book possible.

Many thanks to all of them, including:

Dorothea Jinnah
Karen Strong
Roberto Rivera
Jim Jewell
Martha Walters
David Carlson
Terry White, *Inside Journal*
Judy Kingman
Dan Van Ness
Dell Erwin
Gayle Fitzpatrick
Tom Noton
Joseph Blackmer
Allen Walunga
Ian Howard
Craig Stevenson
Ron Claassen, Center for Conflict Studies and Peacemaking
Howard Zehr, Mennonite Central Committee
Candace Walters
Frank E. Moody, Partners Against Crime
Alison Picard
Ed Tedder, American Probation and Parole Association
Norval Morris
589 prisoners nationwide who wrote letters to Prison
    Fellowship answering the question, "What could
    have stopped you from breaking the law?"

Foreword

We are doing something wrong about crime in America.

Between 1973 and 1992, the population of America's prisons grew from 210,000 to 884,000. We experienced an unprecedented boom in prison construction, costing more than $37 billion. But in spite of the huge number of criminals being imprisoned, our crime rate keeps going up.

Why have we failed to stop crime? Most law-abiding citizens believe it's not their problem. Or, when crime hits close to home, they believe they are powerless to respond. If we continue to believe that somebody else—the police, the FBI, the courts, the psychologists—will take care of crime for us, then we are sadly mistaken.

We need an entirely new way of understanding crime and punishment. For too long, politicians have led us to believe that the best way to deter crime is to lock bad people up, throw away the key, and forget about them. When I served in the Nixon White House, I helped write many of the former president's law-and-order speeches. I helped shape the conservative mentality that has flourished ever since, and I'm not proud of that.

But the liberal view is equally flawed. It excuses criminals of personal responsibility for their actions. Instead of being "bad," criminals are deprived: they are poor, oppressed, uneducated, or discriminated against, so they turn to crime. If this were true, then hundreds of rehabilitation programs focusing only on practical skills would have resulted in an army of reformed ex-convicts taking their places in productive society.

It hasn't happened. When I was a prisoner I watched men spend most of their days lying on their bunks, staring into the emptiness, doing nothing. Prison talk usually centered around how they had gotten caught and how they would avoid it the next time. I've never been in a place so filled with anger, bitterness, despair, and dejection.

It is no wonder to me that after being released, so many ex-prisoners commit new crimes; the wonder is that a substantial number do not.

To deal with the crime crisis, we need a criminal justice policy that charts a third way between liberal and conservative, offering both real punishment and real redemption. That means abandoning the idea altogether that prisons either rehabilitate or deter. Prisons succeed in keeping some violent and dangerous criminals off the street, but beyond that, they accomplish little.

We also need to close the gulf between "us" versus "them." Crime is not just the willful bad behavior of a few misfits; it is a reflection of a crumbling moral consensus about who we are and how we should get along with one another.

The crime problem boils down to concepts that are foreign to our lips today, words that sound quaint—like morality and character. The root of our crime problem is the loss of individual character and the resulting erosion of our character as a people.

If prisons did rehabilitate prisoners, or if the threat of prison deterred crime, surely we would be living in utopian peace. But the stark fact is this: though we've thrown more people in prison than at any other time in human history, one out of four American households will be victimized by crime this year. And every American who pays taxes will continue being victimized by the soaring costs associated with crime.

What can you do to prevent crime where you live? Prison Fellowship, the organization I helped found in 1976 after serving time behind bars myself, has compiled a wealth of ideas in this book. You will be surprised to learn how many of the things described here are easily within your grasp. Most of the suggestions in this book go well beyond crime prevention: they contribute to a better quality of life in your home, your neighborhood, your community.

Ultimately, I believe the solution to our crime problem is a spiritual one. If our goal is individual reformation, and not just institutional reform, this points directly to the essential role of true religious values and true religious hope in our common life. It is the only way to reach into the darkest corners of every community, into the darkest corners of every mind.

The classical Christian message of conversion is what worked in my life, and it is the motivating force behind Prison Fellowship's work nationwide. It is the reason more than 50,000 Prison Fellowship volunteers live their faith by becoming involved in prison ministries. It is a crime prevention program that makes long-term investments in the lives of individuals who cannot simply be written off because they are locked up today.

This book does not try to deal with theories as to what causes criminal behavior and which public policy prescriptions are best. Rather, it is a practical guide to steps each of us can take to keep ourselves and our families safe, to build better relationships within our neighborhoods, and at the same time to consider doing more. How can you help keep young people in school and away from drugs? What could you do to advocate political change on a problem such as gun control or violence on television?

Staying Safe: Prison Fellowship's Guide to Crime Prevention has some good answers you can use. I hope you discover your place in the fight against crime in these pages.

Charles W. Colson

WELCOME HOME
YOUNGER

THE
BIG
PICTURE

*America is a society where crime, sex, violence,
and greed are idolized. If you don't believe me (are you
living in a cave?), just turn your television on, or look
at the top ten video rentals, or the best-selling movies.
We have this crazy affinity with all that is immoral.*

Pete T., Florida

WILL CRIME TOUCH YOUR LIFE?

The bad news

If there are times when you feel vulnerable to crime, you are not alone. A violent crime takes place every seventeen seconds in the United States, and a property crime occurs every two seconds, according to the FBI. Our prison population has quadrupled since 1973, yet in 1991 a record high number of 1.9 million violent crimes were reported to law enforcement agencies.

Factors that are widely viewed as contributing to America's alarming crime rate do not appear to be improving. Family disintegration, racial and ethnic splintering, dwindling urban job opportunities, and a seemingly unstoppable flow of guns and drugs spell more trouble ahead. Experts who track crime agree on at least one thing: the old approaches aren't working. Something radically new is needed.

The good news

Taking precautions to keep crime away from yourself, your home, family, and neighborhood requires some effort, yet many of these suggestions will yield unexpected benefits. They contribute to closer family ties, improved community participation, spruced-up neighborhoods, and camaraderie across the generations.

Once you have gained a measure of confidence about personal security matters, you may wonder what else an individual can do to prevent crime. The suggestions are surprisingly manageable. Preventing crime tomorrow may mean tutoring a drop-out today; it may mean political activism or volunteering to be a Big Brother or Big Sister.

More than a lock

"We must look at crime prevention as more than a lock on the door and a patrol in the street. We must change the entire equation, so that young people do not turn to crime, either in rage or despair, or as a career alternative to school and work" (Roy A. Irving, Chief of Police, Rochester, New York, Speech, June 1992).

A violent nation

"Homicide rates in the United States far exceed those in any other industrialized nation. For other violent crimes, rates in the United States are among the world's highest and substantially exceed rates in Canada, our nearest neighbor in terms of geography, culture, and crime reporting" (National Research Council, *Understanding and Preventing Violence*, ed. Albert J. Reiss, Jr. and Jeffrey A. Roth. [Washington, D.C.: National Academy Press, 1993], 3).

COUNTING THE COST

Certain crimes are measured each year by the FBI's Uniform Crime Reporting Program (UCR). They include crimes of violence and property crimes reported to the FBI by more than 16,000 city, county, and state law enforcement agencies nationwide.

Violent crime

- Aggravated assaults comprised 57 percent of all violent crimes in 1991. A firearm was used in nearly one-fourth of these crimes.

- An average of $817 was taken in each of 1991's 687,732 robberies. In addition, the FBI notes, "While the object of a robbery is to obtain money or property, the crime always involves force or threat of force, and many victims suffer serious personal injury."

- Women reported 106,593 rapes to law enforcement agencies in 1991, a 4 percent increase over 1990.

- Murder took 24,703 lives in 1991. Half of these victims were African-American; 78 percent were male; 89 percent were age 18 or older.

Property crime

"Total dollar losses due to property crime were estimated at $16.1 billion in 1991. The average loss per offense was $1,243" (FBI Uniform Crime Report 1992).

- Nearly one-fourth of all property crimes in 1991 were burglaries. Two out of every three targeted private homes, and burglars struck as often during the daytime as at night.

- Approximately 1 out of every 117 registered motor vehicles was stolen in 1991. It is primarily a big-city problem, worsening in recent years due to carjacking: criminals taking cars forcibly from their drivers.

- Larceny-thefts include pocket-picking, purse-snatching, shoplifting, bicycle thefts, and thefts from buildings, vending machines, and cars. Victims of these crimes lost an estimated $3.9 billion in 1991. And many larceny-thefts go unreported.

- Arson cost property owners an estimated $11,980 per incident in 1991. More than 60 percent of the buildings set on fire were residential and 44 percent were single-family homes.

- Arson offenses also damaged or destroyed commercial property, cars, crops, and timber.

There's more

Crimes not tallied in the FBI's "Crime Index" include forgery, fraud, embezzlement, vandalism, weapons offenses, prostitution, sex offenses, drug abuse violations, gambling, driving under the influence, offenses against family and children, drunkenness, disorderly conduct, vagrancy, and violating liquor, curfew, and loitering laws.

Another source of crime statistics is the U.S. Justice Department's Bureau of Justice Statistics crime survey. Based on a representative sample survey, it indicates that as many as half of all crimes may not be reported to the police.

WHO COMMITS CRIME?

Prison Fellowship began researching this book by publishing a brief notice in *Inside Journal*, our newspaper distributed to prisoners nationwide. In response, 589 prisoners wrote back to answer our question, "What could have stopped you from breaking the law?" You'll find their quotes throughout this book. While the names of these prisoners have been changed, all the excerpts are from real letters. They are not composites.

From their letters, and from research on inmates, a profile emerges that may increase our understanding of who they are. Many prisoners report growing up in homes where abuse and neglect regularly occurred. Those who had more stable homes say they succumbed to peer pressure, to the euphoria of getting easy money illegally, or to their own lack of interest or achievement in school. Others point to frustration brought on by unemployment and extreme family stress. A majority are imprisoned for drug offenses. Addiction and the lure of money kept them coming back for more.

Losing touch

"In the not-so-distant past, many Americans were ill-housed and illiterate, wages were almost universally low, and levels of cyclical unemployment were often extreme. However, crime rates remained low where the traditional agents of social control were strong: families, churches, schools, traditional values, and ethnic solidarity. Crime problems became worse when those agents lost their hold on the young. Many urban neighborhoods now are disorganized because the informal control once exerted by families and local institutions has largely disappeared" (Wesley G. Skogan, "Social Change and the Future of Violent Crime," in *Violence in America,* [Sage Publications, 1989], 244).

Learning by watching

"Modern psychological perspectives emphasize that aggressive and violent behavior are learned responses to frustration, that they can also be learned as instruments for achieving goals, and that the learning occurs by observing models of such behavior. Such models may be observed in the family, among peers, elsewhere in the neighborhood, through the mass media, or in violent pornography" (National Research Council, *Understanding and Preventing Violence,* 7).

Habit-forming

My number one problem has been taking things that don't belong to me. . . . (At college) I saw another fellow leaving his room with his robe wrapped around him. I knew that he was headed for the shower and I knew his roommate had already left for the morning. The thought ran through my mind that I could maybe get a little money while he was in the shower. But I tried not to dwell on the idea. I went ahead and got on the elevator, but the idea of some extra money controlled my thoughts. When I got to the bottom floor I turned right back around and took the stairs back up to the fifth floor. I slipped into his room and took several twenty dollar bills from his wallet and a very nice watch. Little or no suspicion was directed towards me so you can imagine that I really enjoyed spending the money. Little events like that got to be a habit. . . . I ended up being arrested and convicted of burglary in three different states. . . .

If you live your life doing things wrong, someday you will pay for your mistakes. There are no easy ways around it. The same people who I saw struggling and going without years ago now have many of the simple things that I want: A home, a family, and they are being good fathers to their children. If somebody had told me (to) just hang in there and live my life the right way, I probably wouldn't have believed it anyway. I was too eager to get what I wanted right then. But after coming to the Penitentiary they have made a believer out of me.

Leonard C., Tennessee

DO PRISONS KEEP US SAFE?

Prison is often seen as the end of the road for a criminal who is caught, tried, and convicted. Yet most prisoners eventually are released. What have they learned in prison? Sadly, it is a well-documented fact that the main opportunity prison life affords is a chance to learn more about committing crime and "getting even."

Today, more than 880,000 people are in prison in the United States—a 160-percent increase from 1980. Approximately half of all prisoners gain release each year. Beyond prison, 61 percent of offenders are on probation, according to the National Institute of Corrections. Probation officers frequently carry such heavy caseloads that many of their charges get off easy.

Vacuum

"Between overcrowded prisons and even more overcrowded probation, there is a near-vacuum of appropriate and enforced middle-range punishments. . . ." (Norval Morris and Michael Tonry, *Between Prison and Probation* [New York: Oxford University Press, 1990], 14).

Holding pens

"(M)ost of the burden for assuring public safety has been placed on the criminal justice system. But the chief result has been to stretch that system's resources to the breaking point. . . . As we look toward 2000, we must work to create a justice system that, while efficient and secure, also takes seriously the task of preparing offenders for a productive role in society. But, as long as we use the prisons indiscriminately as holding pens for offenders with widely varying needs, that kind of system will not be achieved" (Elliott Currie, *What Kind of Future? Violence and Public Safety in the Year 2000,* [National Council on Crime and Delinquency, July 1987] 19, 21).

Two views from inside

These prisons are like a movie I once seen, where this cave man was frozen in ice for millions of years, (then) one day they thaw him out and he was left to face a world he doesn't understand and doesn't have the slightest clue where to start. Well, that is what they are doing to most convicts; they arrest us, freeze us, and thaw us out. The world is years ahead of us and we are only more acrimonious and confused.

Donald R., California

I'm 28 years old and this is my third time in the prison system. My crimes range from car theft and burglary to assault and battery with intent to kill, kidnapping, and robbery. Each time I was released from prison my crimes increased in violence.

School shows you you can have something if you want it bad enough, but you have to work for it. You have to earn it. I thought I'd have things the easy way, the fast way. I didn't want to end up like my mom, poor with a house full of kids to feed. I've ended up in worse shape, but that's another story.

Chuck K., Oklahoma

What people really want

"A national poll conducted by The Wirthlin Group found that four out of five Americans favor community corrections programs over incarceration for non-dangerous offenders" (Kay Pranis and Mark Umbreit, *Public Opinion Research Challenges Perception of Widespread Public Demand for Harsher Punishment* [Citizens Council monograph, October 1992], 3).

WHAT PRISONERS SAY WOULD STOP CRIME

- **From California:** *If we as a society would stop glamorizing crime by making it seem the hip thing to do to be a gangster, drug dealer, etc., we could show crime as it really is: a very cruel and ruthless game. Show it to these young kids coming up here now in the real light—the light of a prison cell.*

- **From Pennsylvania:** *What could have stopped me is a talk group for burglars. There's no such thing that I know of. If I could have called someone from a talk group I could've been talked out of what I did. Most people (who) rob places are usually depressed. What I did was to take it out on some rich people.*

- **From California:** *When I was 18 I was sent to prison for three years. I tried like hell to get into a drug program but had no luck. . . . Now I'm back with a new term. . . . I'm really scared to get out this time. I'll make it at first, I always do, but then I seem to get sucked into it all over again! That's the only reason I break the law—to get money for my drug problem. But who can help? No one seems to know (or care).*

- **From Florida:** *I think the simple things such as more education and awareness . . . along with more concerted community level involvement could drastically reduce recidivism. We will never stop crime totally, but I believe it can be greatly reduced if enough people get involved.*

Has anyone ever thought of a Big Brother/Big Sister type program for ex-felons?

- **From New York:** *Maybe the best deterrent for me would have been to think that someone really cared.... Most kids (get started in) crime because they want to be accepted by their friends.... What about ex-cons going to schools and talking?... I've thought about talking in schools and maybe acting in a play for kids; I feel that this may help kids more than any Hollywood movie.*

- **From Colorado:** *I am doing time in prison for a sex offense against a child. I believe that the first step in stopping a crime against a child from happening again is admitting that you or whomever has a problem sexually. I came to the place where I had to admit that I cannot control myself sexually especially when it comes to children. ... The second thing is to get help for the problem. There are mental health groups that deal specifically with sex offenders.... Being in a mental health group with others who have committed similar offenses also helps the sex offender to see the problem he has and why he committed the sex offense. ... Mental health programs deal with ways to replace those distorted thoughts with positive ones when those wrong thoughts start and before (they lead) to sexual abuse.*

- **From Mississippi:** *We have good colleges in our prisons today and many of us on the inside pursue careers, yet we cannot get experience. ... Work-release is fine for the laborer, but for the college graduate-inmate there is not a pre-release program that helps him gain the experience necessary to be a productive member of society.... Some of us are career-oriented and need help along these lines.*

WHY SHOULD I GET INVOLVED?

"Statistics tell the story. Police and sheriffs' departments in cities, small towns, and suburbs throughout the country report substantial decreases in crime due to citizens' self-help education and preventive efforts" (National Crime Prevention Council, *Community Crime Prevention: An Organizer's Handbook*).

Kids need to know

"A child's best response to trouble is using common sense. Like knowing when to stick up for his or her rights, and when not to. Small children should not fight back when outnumbered by bigger youths who want to take their bike, radio, or other possession. In this situation, a child should give in and then run to an adult, or older brother or sister, and report the incident right away" (McGruff, the Crime Dog).

It's the thing to do

Since Neighborhood Watch began in 1972, sheriffs, police departments and citizen organizations have worked to develop nearly 30,000 separate neighborhood crime prevention programs. More than 15 million people in all 50 states participate in watch programs (The Sign Center, Inc.).

A constructive outlet

Being involved in crime prevention gives citizens a constructive way to channel their anger about crime. Many effective and well-known victim organizations, such as Mothers Against Drunk Driving (MADD), were started by victims or their families.

A victim may need you

"Family, friends, and bystanders are often the first helpers available to respond to a victim. . . . Even if you cannot stop a crime, you can be of great help to the victim immediately afterwards. Often the support and assistance given at that time is critical to the victim's recovery. And later, a victim may need patient listeners to help him talk out his despair at being victimized" (National Organization for Victim Assistance).

Your money, your choice

It costs as much as $20,000 to house one prisoner each year, and another $85,000 just to build the space to house him. And prison construction costs keep rising. Even if you avoid being victimized by crime, you still pay for crime: your tax dollars support a criminal justice system that, experts agree, needs an overhaul.

Where do I begin?

Read this book, which will equip you to:

• Take simple steps at home to enhance your security.

- Get to know your neighbors and work together to protect and improve your surroundings.

- Learn how to respond if crime strikes you or a loved one.

- Discover how changed lives can reduce crime. See if you can help someone make life choices that do not involve breaking the law.

- Consider how cultural, political, and social forces contribute to crime. Let people in power know what you think.

AROUND YOUR HOME

Keep a radio on in the living room or bedroom; have a light set on a timer in the house; have a tape recorder playing a dog's bark; buy a dog and keep it in the house (of course not Snoopy, but Cujo).

Wendell B., Virginia

1. TAKE AN INVENTORY

Write down what you own and mark valuable items with an identifying number. This makes it easier to file an accurate insurance claim if your home is burglarized. Marked property is more readily returned by the police if they recover it. Also, marked items are less valuable to burglars: they'll have a harder time "fencing," or selling, your stolen goods.

- Using the sample inventory on page 35, list your valuables and your credit cards. Make two copies of the list; keep one at home and store the other in a safe deposit box or with a relative.

- Borrow an electric engraver from your local police station and identify items such as your stereo, VCR, home computer, and television with your Social Security or driver's license number, beginning with the state abbreviation. Example: NY 000-00-0000.

- When you mark your valuables and complete an inventory, you are participating in Operation Identification. Most police stations will issue Operation Identification stickers for you to display on your outside doors. People imprisoned for burglary wrote to us saying they would go elsewhere if they knew a homeowner had taken anti-theft precautions.

- If you own a camcorder, shoot some footage of each room in your home, clearly showing the valuables you've listed and engraved. Color snapshots are another option. Store the videotape or photos in a safe deposit box or with a trusted friend or relative.

- Store things that you seldom use in places burglars seldom look. For example, don't keep your best jewelry in a jewelry box; put it in a plain box in a bedroom closet or on a basement shelf.

Sample Property Inventory

Item	Make/ Model	Serial Number	Purchase Date/ Price
Answering machine			
Antiques			
Art objects, paintings			
Battery charger			
Bicycle/Motorcycle			
Binoculars			
Cameras (and other photographic equip.)			
Coins			
Collections			
Computer, printer			
Clocks			
Cutlery			
Golf clubs			
Guns			
Jewelry			
Kitchen appliances (microwave, processor)			

Item	Make/ Model	Serial Number	Purchase Date/ Price
Lawn mower			
Musical instruments			
Office equipment			
Power tools			
Radios			
Stereos			
Sewing machine			
Small hand tools			
Stereo speakers			
Sporting goods			
Tape recorders			
Televisions			
Typewriter			
VCR			
Other			

Credit Cards

Company/ Phone number	Account Number	Credit Limit

2. GET A BURGLAR'S EYE VIEW

Me and a few friends would just cruise around in the country until we thought we saw a house where nobody was home. We would go up and knock, and if nobody answered, we would go on in, while one of the guys would take off in the car and we would tell him to be back in 30 minutes. We always made sure there were woods or a cornfield in case someone came home and we had to run. We would do six or seven a day like it wasn't anything.

Nathaniel S., Indiana

Making your home less burglar-friendly does not mean turning it into a fortress. Begin by taking a look around your home's exterior. Crime-proof it and make it more attractive, too.

- Get out your hedgetrimmer and go after overgrown bushes or tree limbs that hide doors or windows. Check to see whether branches offer access to second-story windows. If they do, cut them back.

- Make sure obscure openings into your home can be secured. These may include a swinging door used by a pet, a crawl space, or a ventilation opening.

- Conquer clutter on your porch and in your yard. Do not allow newspapers or flyers to accumulate near your front door or on the driveway. Put away tools, toys, bikes, or equipment that might lure a burglar into your yard.

- Avoid advertising your family's name. Don't display it on a welcome mat or mailbox because a would-be burglar could use it to get your telephone number and call to see if you are home. Likewise, a con artist or child molester who knows your name and address could more easily compel you or your children to listen to his ruse.

- Light up your life. Each exterior door should be well-lit, and so should your house number. Use a timer inside your home to turn on a porch light at dusk and turn it off late at night or at dawn. These are available at hardware or do-it-yourself stores; they attach to the wallplate that operates your porch light.

- Consider installing outside floodlights just below your roofline to illuminate a dark driveway or side yard. Or use an energy-saving motion detection device, which turns on a floodlight immediately if there is any movement in your yard or driveway. Call your local electric power company to see if they have a program to install security lighting.

- Ask your local police department for a free "security survey." A trained officer will visit your home and evaluate how its security may be improved. Tell your neighbors to do the same!

3. LOCK UP

Make it a habit to keep doors and windows locked, no matter how quickly you'll be back home. Burglars assume (often correctly) that houses sit empty all day. And police estimate that as often as forty percent of the time, burglars just walk right in.

Doors

- The safest type of exterior door is made of metal, steel, or solid-core wood. A hollow-core door, made of thin wood over a wood frame, can be kicked in or pulled apart by a determined burglar. Likewise, a door with glass window panes makes your home more vulnerable. A sliding glass door should be secured with a tight-fitting metal or wooden dowel and a keyed lock.

- Have a peephole installed in your front door, and never open the door to a stranger. If someone knocks, check identification.

- Be sure to secure the door from your garage into your house. Thieves will use the cover of a garage to gain entry undetected.

- Don't rely only on the locking mechanism which is standard on most exterior doors. On its own, it does not secure your home from easy entry by a burglar.

Some door manufacturers offer an anti-shim device, which prevents a plastic card from opening the latch.

- The best door lock is a deadbolt lock. There are three basic types:

  1. **A double-cylinder deadbolt** operates by key both inside and outside. Don't leave the inside key in the lock; hang it on a nail in a nearby closet.

  2. **A single-cylinder tubular deadbolt** is operated by key from the outside only. Inside, you turn a knob to move the deadbolt.

  3. **Rim-mounted locks** are installed on the door's inside surface. They are easy to install, less expensive, and offer good security. They come with either a vertical or horizontal bolt.

- Check the strike plate, which holds the bolt in place when the door is locked. Replace thin-gauge metal strike plates with heavy-duty ones. Anchor them with #12 three-inch wood screws.

- Never leave a key to your home in a "secret" outdoor hiding place. Burglars know exactly where to look for "hidden" keys. Give a house key to a trusted neighbor instead.

Windows

- Pay close attention to basement windows that may offer easy entry to burglars. Replace regular pane glass windows with plexiglass or polycarbonate. Consider using security bars, a heavy-duty screen, or ornamental grillwork for added protection.

- Check the latches on **casement windows** to be sure they work properly. The crank handle should feel tight, not wiggly. On first-floor windows that are seldom opened, consider removing the handle and storing it in a nearby drawer. If someone breaks the glass, they will not be able to open the window.

- **Louvered windows** (which open out like awnings) are very difficult to secure. Think about removing them and replacing them with solid glass.

- **Double-hung windows** can be crime-proofed by drilling a hole that angles downward through a top corner of the bottom window into the bottom of the top window. Place a dowel pin or nail into the hole to keep the window shut.

- **Sliding windows** are best protected by a metal or wooden bar, just the same as a sliding glass door. To prevent these windows from being lifted out of their tracks, drill a hole through the top of the window frame and insert a steel pin or nail.

- Practice undoing your window and door locks so no one will be trapped inside in case of fire or other emergency. Be sure your children can operate the locks as well. Establish a family fire escape plan and schedule a "drill."

- If you spend a lot of time away from home, consider installing a security system. Burglars avoid homes identified by signs or stickers announcing an alarm system. These systems have become increasingly popular and prices have come down. Both wired and wireless systems are available. Call your police department for recommendations.

I have been a burglar most of my life. I'm presently doing a 20-year sentence. . . . Two weeks after my arrest I became a Christian. Several months later my cell was shook down. For some reason the guards took everything and scattered it all over the floor, including my sheets and blanket. When I walked in to straighten everything up, I saw and realized how all my victims must have felt when they came home after I burglarized them. I felt so ashamed and I knew then I would never do it again.

Robert L., Kentucky

For a comprehensive discussion of interior security, see *How to Protect Yourself From Crime* by Ira A. Lipman (Chicago: Contemporary Books, 1989).

4. "I'M NOT AT HOME RIGHT NOW...."

With just a little sleight-of-hand, you can make your home appear occupied when it is not.

If you'll be back soon

- Maintain a lived-in look by leaving some lights on and a radio tuned to a talk show.

- Leave your telephone answering machine on all the time. Be sure your message does *not* say, "I'm not at home right now." Instead, say something like this: "You have reached (your telephone number). No one can answer this call now, but please leave your name, number, and a brief message. We will get back to you shortly."

- If you have a garage door, close and lock it.

- Do not post notes on your doors giving information about where you are or when you will return. If you need to get a message to a delivery person or family member, ask a neighbor to watch for them.

- Ask a friend to stay in your house if you need to attend a family wedding or funeral that has been announced in advance in the newspaper.

If you're gone several days or longer

- Stop delivery of your mail and newspaper by contacting the post office and newspaper office directly. Consider Call Forwarding, a telephone company service allowing your calls to ring through to the number where you'll be staying.

- Ask a friend or neighbor to keep an eye on your house and yard while you are gone. They can help you by placing a trash can or garbage bag in front of your house on collection day and by collecting flyers or deliveries that may accumulate on your front porch or driveway. Do the same for your neighbors when they go away.

- Set lights and radios on timers so your house looks occupied after dark. Leave shades and draperies in their usual daytime position so the house does not look "shut down."

- Arrange to have your lawn mowed regularly.

- Avoid talking about your travel plans in public; don't permit your travel schedule to be published, even in an office or church newsletter.

- Get a housesitter whom you know and trust to live at your home while you are away.

5. DON'T GET CONNED

Con artists stalk you right where you live, through your telephone, your mail, and advertisements in newspapers and magazines. A Louis Harris poll estimates telemarketing thieves have made contact with nine out of ten Americans. How can you avoid being conned?

- Take your time. If someone is offering a legitimate business opportunity, product, service, or prize, you will not be pressured into making a "snap" decision. Insist on seeing documented evidence of what is being described and check references carefully.

- Never reveal your credit card number over the phone. Swindlers often call and say you've won a free gift or an expensive vacation. In order to collect the prize, all you need to do is verify your charge card number. Don't buy it! Once you've given out your credit card number, anyone who has it can make purchases by phone and charge your account.

- Guard your *telephone* credit card number closely as well, especially when placing a call from a public telephone. Cases of computer bulletin boards listing telephone credit card numbers have resulted in many charged calls to unsuspecting victims. This is a particular problem in areas where drug dealers call foreign suppliers, using stolen numbers to cover their tracks.

- If it *sounds* too good to be true, it probably *is*. Be suspicious of schemes promising you will "get rich quick." Newspaper ads beguile readers into thinking they can earn good money working at home. You are asked to pay up front for supplies or an instruction book. Later, you discover there is no market for what you are supposed to produce, or your work is not "up to our standards." The money you invested is never refunded. And you earn nothing.

- The American Association of Retired Persons (AARP) says older citizens are victimized by con artists to a much greater extent than younger individuals. Be skeptical about claims of miracle cures, cheap glasses or hearing aids, investment opportunities, charitable giving opportunities, and special deals on home repairs. If you feel uncertain or confused, call someone you trust.

- Before you buy property, go and see it. Ask whether improvements and services such as utilities, water, and sewage disposal are included. Find out the going rental rates in the neighborhood and never assume a vacation property or time share will increase in value.

- Insist that charitable organizations provide written evidence of their purpose, use of funds, and tax deductibility. It's best to give money to organizations you know and trust.

- Know a con game when you see one. The National Crime Prevention Council (NCPC) says these are the classics:

  1. **The pigeon drop.** Strangers tell you they've found a large sum of money. They'll split their good fortune with you if you put up some "good faith" money. You turn over the cash, and you never hear from them again.

  2. **Bank examiner fraud.** A "bank official" asks you to help him catch a dishonest teller. You must withdraw money from your account and turn it over to him. You do, and you never see your money again. No real official would ask you to participate in a scheme like this.

  3. **Funeral chaser.** Shortly after a relative dies, someone delivers to your door a leather-bound Bible which the deceased supposedly ordered. Or you receive a bill in the mail for an expensive item on which you must make the remaining payments. The "funeral chaser" uses obituary notices to defraud bereaved families. You are not responsible for anyone else's purchases; if a legitimate claim comes to light, it will be settled by the estate.

  4. **Pyramid scheme.** It sounds like a painless way to make money: you invest a certain amount of cash and solicit others to do the same. When the pyramid crashes—as it always does—everyone loses except the person at the top who has kept the money and never invested it.

If you are the victim of a con game or fraud, tell someone:

- Call your police department and ask if they have a consumer fraud unit.

- Write a letter to the editor of your local newspaper. Tell the Chamber of Commerce and the Better Business Bureau.

- Contact the National Fraud Information Center at the National Consumers League, 815 15th Street, N.W., Suite 928-N, Washington, D.C. 20005. 202-639-8140 or 1-800-876-7060.

- Get in touch with Call for Action, 3400 Idaho Ave. N.W., Suite 101, Washington, D.C. 20016.

- Warn your neighbors and friends.

Practice saying these lines:

"I must talk this over with a professional/relative."
"No, thank you. I am not interested."
"Let me think about it for a few days."
"Send me more information."

6. PLAY THE WHAT-IF GAME

If you are a parent, few things matter more than keeping your children safe. The place to begin is at home, teaching them what to do and how to get help if they feel threatened.

- Even precocious preschoolers can play the "what-if" game. Begin a dialogue with your children that helps them consider what to do in a situation where they may not feel safe.

   Ask questions such as, "What if someone offered you candy to get in a car?" "What if a bigger kid takes something from you?" "What if we went to the mall and you couldn't find Mommy or Daddy?" Continue this sort of conversation through the years.

- Teach children to dial 911 or the emergency number in your community. Have them practice on a toy telephone. By the time they enter first grade, they should be able to recite full name, address, and telephone number.

- *Do not* tell your child, "Never talk to strangers." Instead, tell them not to *listen to* or *go with* any stranger who approaches them or offers them something. Children tend to think a "stranger" is a scary-looking person whose evil intent is plain for all to see. The truth is, bad guys often don't look "bad," and they might not be strangers at all. A child in trouble may need to seek help from a "good stranger"—a shop keeper, police officer, or bus driver. Assure your child that most people are friendly and safe.

- Tell your children you will never send a stranger to pick them up at school or at play. Anyone who tells a child, "your mom sent me" is telling a lie. The child should run away immediately.

- When your children are old enough to be out on their own, buy them simple, easy-to-read watches to keep track of time.

- Have children "sign out" before they leave the house, noting where they are going and what time they expect to return.

- If your child is home alone, review these rules:

  1. Never open the door to someone you do not know.

  2. Never tell someone on the phone your name or address.

  3. Never tell a caller you are home alone. Say, "My mom (or dad) can't come to the phone right now."

  4. Let your child practice locking and unlocking the doors.

- Explain the difference between "good touch" and "bad touch." Teach children that hugs, kisses and "roughhousing" are usually fine among family members and good friends, as long as they do not feel overwhelmed or afraid. It is okay for a doctor or nurse to examine a child's body. It is *not* okay for anyone to play "secret" games with a child's body or to touch a child in a way that makes the child uncomfortable.

About that child molester out on the prowl: Do not give him the opportunity. Make it impossible for him to succeed by making his intended victim—your child—too smart and aware.

This is my fourth period of incarceration. . . . I made a lot of poor choices, mostly because I simply didn't care about anybody else or anything else. The crimes that I'm in prison for today range from burglary to operating a vehicle without the owner's permission to disorderly conduct and several counts of sexual assault of children.

If a child tells his parents . . . that he was molested, someone should believe him! Too many children to count, after they are molested (like myself), are threatened that something serious will happen if they tell. I was seven years old when I was molested by my step-father, and I was told, "If you tell your mom, I'll splatter your brains all over the road."

Luke R., Wisconsin

More than 75 percent of child sexual abuse is done by a person the parent knows and trusts ("How to Raise a Street-Smart Child" from HBO Video).

7. TREAT ALCOHOL AND DRUGS RESPONSIBLY

I grew up with a mom (who) was alcoholic. . . . I used to sneak some of her whiskey and drink it . . . because it made me feel like I was grown up. Boy, was I ever wrong, huh? Anyway, I started hanging around with guys who used to stay out all night drinking and robbing houses. I went with my so-called friends and broke into my first house. I saw how easy it was to make a lot of money real fast and I couldn't keep a steady job because of my drinking, so I took the easy way out and started stealing for a living. I didn't care about getting caught; just that I had enough money to get drunk with.

I thought that I had things under control and that I could quit drinking anytime I wanted to. But my drinking took everything from me—my family, freedom, girlfriend. I was out of control. It took prison for me to learn that.

Larry A., Florida

- Even if you do not drink, you still must discuss drinking and drug use with your children. They will meet with peer pressure early and often.

- Set family rules that can help your child say no: "My parents won't let me get my driver's license this year if I mess around with alcohol or drugs."

- Tell your children exactly what drinking and drug use will do to them. Physical effects may include slowed growth, impaired coordination, diminished fertility, soaring heart rates that may be lethal, and addiction. Mentally, your child may lose control and good judgment; he may experience memory loss, an inability to concentrate, and he may no longer be motivated. He may lose friends and feel disconnected. More detailed information is available from your public library, police station, and local chapter of MADD or SADD (Students Against Drunk Driving).

• If you drink alcohol, set a responsible example: don't drink alone, drink moderate amounts that do not make you drunk, and don't make alcohol use a regular habit. Never drink and drive! If you serve alcohol, be sure to provide nonalcoholic beverages as well for guests who prefer them.

• It is against the law to serve alcohol to minors. The National Crime Prevention Council points out that it is crucial for parents to communicate clearly the fact that they will not accept drinking or drug use by their children.

According to the National Institute of Justice, adolescents most often begin using drugs and alcohol between the ages of 13 and 15:

"The primary factors that promote use are the general availability of alcohol or drugs, friends who are users, lack of parental supervision, and lack of attachment to school. . . . Over 75 percent of boys who use alcohol and marijuana commit minor assaults, vandalism, or other public disorder offenses. . . . Girls are more likely to be involved in more covert property crimes, such as shoplifting and petty theft. "

Many of the prisoner letters we've received recount the horror of drug addiction. They often affirm the value of examples set by parents. What a parent says can help counteract the myths young people believe, such as "everyone's doing it," "I won't get addicted," and "it will make me feel great." Two letters from inmates paint a different picture:

Initially cocaine made me feel better about myself. . . . My social use evolved into a full-blown habit over a period of two years. If I was to be stopped, it should have been then. I began dealing on small levels to support my ever-increasing need for the drug. During this time I probably could have been stopped if somebody cared enough to force me into a rehab program. But since addicts tend to hang with other addicts—the drug being the only common denominator—who's gonna help?

As my dependency increased so did my dealing. My "group" became seedier and more dangerous. Guns started coming into the picture, and although I'd never had a use or even a fascination for firearms, they were a new-found symbol of power; part of the image, part of the game.

Hank D., California

I am currently under a sentencing obligation of 70 years . . . for two counts of first-degree murder, (but) I am in prison because of drugs.

I started out in high school selling pot or weed to friends. . . . Other kids looked up to me, so I thought it was cool. Not long after that, I was introduced to cocaine. Just with the little bit I was dealing I would often have over $1,000 in my pocket. . . .

Other kids in school saw me loaded with money all the time, and they really looked up to me. I would have three or four cars at a time. I would get tired of driving a certain car, so I would just give it to a friend of mine in school. Then I just dropped school altogether, because everybody knew who and what I was.

. . . . Next I was introduced to big dealers and bigger-money buyers. I got my own condominium in southwest Houston, and put a lot of my friends to work dealing my dope. They were more than willing to get the fame and fortune I was acquiring. I had ten high school friends dealing dope for me. Six of those ten are dead now because of me. Three are in prison. The one who was left got out before it was too late. Smart move!

Next thing I knew, I put myself in the position of kill or be killed. So I will spend 22 years day for day in prison thinking about the lives I took control of and destroyed. There are times when I just don't think I can bear another day, and the only thing I would like to do is change what happened.

Ben O., Texas

8. HUG YOUR KIDS

To commit a crime, a criminal needs two things: an opportunity and a victim who appears vulnerable. Taking safety precautions around your home reduces the opportunity; building positive self-esteem in your children makes it less likely that they will be victimized or drawn into criminal activity.

The child who feels good about himself probably will not be the "loner" on the playground or find himself attracted to gangs or cults. Studies have shown that children who value themselves are also more likely to refuse alcohol and drugs. They tend to care about doing well in school and they make friends with kids who share similar values.

At the same time, it's important to keep in mind that children are individuals with the freedom to choose. No matter how skilled and loving a parent may be, other influences will shape a child's life. Don't blame yourself for every wrong choice a child makes.

- Good parenting skills don't come naturally—they are learned. Subscribe to a magazine on parenting and read books about child development. Join a parents' support group or take a class. Knowing what to expect from your children as they grow is a first step toward assuring good mental health.

- Demonstrate unconditional love for your children by telling them they are loved and valued just for being who they are. Children of all ages need your affection.

- Praise your children for effort as well as accomplishment. Help them understand that trying is as important as winning.

- Discipline your children consistently and fairly. Set limits they understand. When you need to correct, focus on the child's action, not the child's character. Say, "Crossing the street without looking was a dangerous thing to do," rather than "How could you be so stupid, running across the street that way?"

- Teach empathy to your children, one prisoner recommended, by taking them to a home for the elderly or even an animal shelter. A sense of altruism and a caring attitude need to be modeled and taught.

- Make each child a valued family "team member." As soon as they are old enough, give them some responsibilities around the house. Taking charge of routine tasks gives them a sense of accomplishment and belonging.

- Teach your children to settle disputes with words, not fights or weapons. Model behavior that helps your children avoid schoolyard bullies and defuse potentially threatening encounters.

  > "By seeing adults express anger *without losing control*, kids learn that anger is not too dangerous or too overwhelming to face, to feel, and to let go of" (Deborah Prothrow-Stith, M.D.,

Deadly Consequences [New York: HarperCollins 1991], 130–31).

• Do your best to prevent your children from having access to printed pornography as well as violent and sexually explicit television programs or videos when you're not home or when they visit friends.

If parents would take the time to talk to their children, pay attention to any problems they may have, and be good listeners without yelling or judging, a lot of juvenile crimes, alcohol abuse, and drug abuse would be prevented. Children and adults usually only need someone to talk to; someone whom they can trust and confide in; someone (to) give guidance to their problems. But when they don't get what they need, they do something to call attention to themselves. . . .

I'm 21 years old. I'm in on a second-degree felony of kidnapping. I have committed many crimes . . . for which I have never been caught. Most of them occurred in my early teens.

Anne Y., Utah

9. GET HELP NOW FOR FAMILY CONFLICTS

Many factors contribute to violence in the home: a history of family abuse, alcoholism or drug addiction, depression, stress from joblessness or marital conflict. Just because domestic violence can be explained does not mean it can be excused. It is a crime. Yet the cycle of family violence can be broken. Help is available.

- In 1992, 1,261 children died from abuse or neglect. Reported cases of child abuse that year numbered 2.9 million, according to The National Committee to Prevent Child Abuse (NCPCA). Family violence also erupts between spouses, between siblings, and toward elderly relatives.

- Most of the time, children who suffer physical, sexual, or emotional abuse are victimized by family members. In a recent survey, the NCPCA found that fewer than two percent of reported abuse cases take place in foster care or child care settings.

  "Victims of family violence exhibit depression, suicidal feelings, self-contempt, and an inability to trust and to develop intimate relationships" ("Family Violence: An Overview," U.S. Department of Health and Human Services, National Center on Child Abuse and Neglect, January 1991, 18).

- Compared with other children, child victims of severe violence are more likely to have failing grades and disciplinary problems in school, to have difficulty forming friendships, to imitate assaultive behaviors, to engage in vandalism and theft, and to use alcohol and drugs ("Family Violence: An Overview," 19).

- Before family difficulties escalate, seek assistance from one or more of the following resources in your area: community mental health centers, private mental health clinics, or trained psychotherapists, including psychologists, psychiatrists, pastoral counselors, or licensed clinical social workers.

For additional help, contact:

Parents Anonymous
520 S. Lafayette Park Place
Suite 316
Los Angeles, CA 90057
213-388-6685

Crimes in society happen in part due to lack of a person's touch with shared or collective reality and due to irrational thinking and decision-making. Because criminals have not learned to challenge their individual perceptions, borne out of sin but more specifically irrational core beliefs (that may have been cultivated in the bed of dysfunctional families), stress in life is not handled well except through alcohol, drugs, sex and violence, or any other criminally conditioned response.

Mitch G., Minnesota

AROUND YOUR COMMUNITY

My main job was breaking and entering into houses and offices. What I've noticed most about the houses I have hit is that the community they are in lacks concerned people. I noticed none of my victims lived in a crime watch district. I understand there are crime watch programs around, and people should be more alert about these.

Tom L., Maine

10. HOST A BLOCK PARTY

Getting acquainted with your neighbors not only helps stop crime—it's fun and everyone can participate. Neighbors who develop friendships and become attuned to comings and goings will notice when something out of the ordinary happens. And the fear of crime diminishes when you know others are looking out for you.

- Plan a backyard social event and invite all the neighbors. Enlist help with food preparation, set up, and clean up. The event could be focused around a theme such as a children's bike parade, the Fourth of July, or Labor Day.

- Ask neighbors to write their names, addresses, and phone numbers on a list; type and copy the list and distribute a neighborhood directory. The directory could also include children's names and ages.

- If you establish a neighborhood association with regular events and meetings, consider ways to reward positive behavior as well as looking for suspicious behavior. For instance, the association could appoint someone just to say thanks to neighbors who pick up litter or tend plants in common areas.

- The association could recruit able-bodied neighbors to assist elderly or disabled residents with home security projects.

- Invite a police spokesperson to visit your association and discuss neighborhood safety.

"Ultimately, promoting social interaction and fighting isolation may be the most effective weapon against crime" (NCPC, "Community Crime Prevention: An Organizer's Handbook").

11. ORGANIZE A NEIGHBORHOOD WATCH

Millions of people participate in Neighborhood Watch programs nationwide. These programs encourage and train people to observe and report suspicious and criminal activity to police. By doing so, you can dramatically decrease the incidence of crime where you live.

- Start a watch program by inviting your neighbors to meet with a local police spokesperson. He or she will explain how the program works in your area. Usually, you must meet requirements such as participation by half of all available households and a commitment to some crime-prevention training. Then you will be eligible for official Neighborhood Watch signs to be installed.

- Choose a coordinator and block captains. Each block captain contacts nearby neighbors to enlist their help and keep them informed. The coordinator prepares and hands out a neighborhood map including names, addresses, and telephone numbers for every household.

- Emphasize that Neighborhood Watch participants are not vigilantes, taking the law into their own hands. The only responsibility you have is to call the police and report what you see or hear. The police will respond and intervene if necessary.

- Organize teams to patrol the neighborhood on foot, on bicycles, or in cars at times when your neighborhood may be most vulnerable.

- What to watch for: A stranger entering a neighbor's home; anyone peering into parked cars; suspicious sounds such as a scream or breaking glass; people loitering around playgrounds or parks; moving vans or other trucks pulling up at an unoccupied house.

- Schedule regular meetings (perhaps four times each year) to provide updates, generate enthusiasm, and recognize individuals for outstanding participation. The meetings may also focus on issues such as self-defense, drug abuse, and child safety. Some programs publish a newsletter or sell promotional items such as mugs or tee shirts.

In Tennessee, a group called Memphis Area Neighborhood Watch, Inc., has grown into a multifaceted non-profit corporation supported by private and state grants. It hosts an annual awards celebration to honor outstanding local crime-prevention efforts. It is the primary sponsor in a coalition of law enforcement agencies and businesses of the area's participation in National Night Out. The group publishes a newsletter, maintains a speakers' list, and provides information and referral services to the approximately 1,200 Neighborhood Watch groups. In a low-income housing complex, Memphis Area Neighborhood Watch initiated a Violence Reduction Project funded by the Tennessee Department of Health. The project teaches children ages 5 to 17 how to resolve disputes without violence and assists them in boosting reading skills, avoiding drug use, and maintaining physical and mental health.

Family Data Sheet

Address _____

Telephone _____

Homeowner(s) Name_____

Children_____Age_____

_____Age_____

Other Residents_____

Work Telephone Numbers _____

Individual to contact in case of emergency:

Name_____

Telephone_____

Family Vehicles:

Year/Make	Style	Color	License #

Family Medical Difficulties_____

Special Training, Skills_____

Persons Authorized to Enter Home
(babysitter, housecleaner)

Name_____

Day of Week_____Approx Time_____

12. BLOCK PARTY? BUT I LIVE IN AN APARTMENT!

Traditional watch programs have been adapted to multi-family dwellings where tenants come and go. Neighborhood Watch is based on building relationships among neighbors over time. That's a good idea for apartment-dwellers, too, but often it is not possible. Apartment Watch takes a different tack: it equips and encourages complex managers to get the crime-prevention message out to residents. Using these tips from the Orlando, Florida, police department, tell your apartment manager what he or she can do:

- Ask a police officer to conduct a survey of the building and make recommendations. The manager must agree to an annual follow-up survey to check additions or renovations.

- Require new tenants to view a video, supplied by police, which explains Apartment Watch and offers crime prevention tips.

- Hold at least two crime prevention seminars each year, geared toward specific needs. For instance, if auto thefts have increased, a seminar could explore ways to prevent car theft.

- Include crime prevention tips, supplied regularly by the police department, in newsletters or on bulletin boards.

- Incorporate Apartment Watch guidelines into procedural manuals to keep the program alive when a manager is replaced.

13. EXPAND YOUR HORIZONS

Beyond your Watch program, there are a number of creative ways to keep interest high, to involve more people, and to spread the word about crime prevention:

- Keep an eye out for new information about home security and distribute it to your Neighborhood Watch participants. Have crime prevention materials translated into Spanish or another language used widely by immigrants in your area.

- Participate in National Night Out, an annual anti-crime event sponsored by the National Association of Town Watch. Since 1984, National Night Out has grown to involve more than 23 million people in the United States, Canada, and on military bases worldwide.

  Scheduled for the first Tuesday in August, National Night Out encourages neighbors to get acquainted and take part in special events focusing on safety and community solidarity against crime. For information, contact National Association of Town Watch, P.O. Box 303, Wynnewood, PA 19096 or call 215-649-7055.

- Cooperate with other groups in your community by sharing resources and promotion around events focusing on goals such as child safety and neighborhood beautification.

- Encourage a few watchers to volunteer to keep an eye on neighborhood maintenance. They can call in reports of burned-out street lights, missing road signs, and abandoned cars.

- Tell utility workers or delivery people who serve your community about your program. Recruit them to act as auxiliary watchers.

- Ask banks and other local businesses to include crime prevention materials when they mail statements or bills.

- Hold a crime-prevention fair at a local shopping center or mall.

- Take the initiative to demonstrate your respect for the law: Leave handicapped parking places for those who really need them; treat other people's property with respect; keep your pets under control. Show by your actions that the little things matter!

- Get involved when you see criminal activity by reporting it to the police and volunteering to testify, if needed, in court.

One grassroots community effort that goes beyond Neighborhood Watch is the Westside Crime Prevention Program (WCPP) on Manhattan's upper west side. The group conducts Drug Watch Training Sessions, enabling merchants, churches, schools, and others to work together to shut down open-air drug markets. They distribute yellow "Safe Haven" stickers to store owners willing to help children in need. WCPP staffs a community help line for people reporting a crime or needing help after a crime has occurred. And the group serves as a link between the community, local police department, substance abuse treatment centers, and other groups working for safer neighborhoods.

14. COPE CREATIVELY WITH NEIGHBORHOOD CONFLICT

Outsiders are not the only source of trouble in a neighborhood. Sometimes conflict erupts among neighbors over irritants such as barking dogs, loud parties, or teenagers hanging around. Keeping the peace means early intervention, before a situation escalates out of control.

- If conflict breaks out, the investment you've already made in neighborhood organizing will pay off. It is much easier to work out a solution with people you know.

- Get training on how to resolve conflict using cooperative strategies. Call the Center for Conflict Studies at Fresno Pacific College, 209-453-2064.

- Go directly to the person who's causing the difficulty or, if it's a child, to the parent. Avoid the temptation to talk behind the person's back and gossip about the problem with other neighbors. That only spreads the frustration further.

- When you talk to the person, listen to his or her point of view. The goal is to work out an accommodation that meets everyone's needs, not just yours.

- If you need outside help or if the person poses a danger to himself, his family, or anyone else, call the police. If you resort to this option too quickly or too often, however, recognize that police intervention may create additional problems. A neighbor who chronically gets a police visit when the neighbors complain is apt to grow embarrassed and enraged.

- When you confront a person who is disturbing the neighborhood, be prepared: he or she may be hostile and uncooperative. On the other hand, you may be pleasantly surprised—often when a neighbor cares enough to confront in person, the response is more thoughtful and compromise more likely.

15. JOIN FORCES WITH THE POLICE

Pairs of officers on bicycles patrol Fairfax County, VA, in an area crowded with recent immigrants from Latin America. One officer on each of two teams speaks Spanish fluently. These "neighborhood police units" help residents with basic social services as well as protection from crime. They discovered a couple living in an apartment that had no heat, and they contacted the right authorities to get the problem fixed. Often, they are more effective than motorized patrols because no one hears them coming. Two officers made a drug arrest when they saw two people sitting in a car parked behind a shopping center. They rode up silently on their bikes and observed the couple using cocaine (Adapted from Leonard Hughes, "Putting Their Mettle to the Pedal," *Washington Post*, 4 February, 1993).

• Ask about community policing where you live. Traditional police work involves car patrols, rapid response to calls for help, and investigating crimes that have been committed. Community policing takes a different, preventive approach. Individual officers build working relationships with local merchants and people in schools. They troubleshoot local problems, offer guidance on crime prevention, and intervene when needed to protect the neighborhood.

- Visit your police department and get to know the people and procedures that affect your community. Find out when the station is open for tours by school groups or neighborhood groups. Invite the police to participate in community events by issuing children's identification cards and taking their fingerprints.

- Invite a police spokesperson to your community group, school or church to speak on crime prevention and neighborhood cooperation.

- See if your police department sponsors summer sports activities for children. Volunteer your time to help out.

In Seattle, community policing "has enabled the community and the police to work together on a day-to-day basis in the joint task of controlling crime and increasing public security. Together, citizens and police define the problems, select the targets to be addressed, and in many cases share in developing the strategies to deal with them. . . . The partnership has provided benefits for both parties that sustain and reinforce the relationship between the police and the community. When citizens feel more safe and secure, and when police experience the support of citizens who lobby for better legislation and more resources for police work, the partnership is continually reinforced" (From "A Model Partnership Between Citizens and Police," in *National Institute of Justice Journal*, August 1992, 18).

16. STAY SAFE AWAY FROM HOME

You may feel secure at home and in your neighborhood, but what can you do to take that sense of security with you when you leave familiar turf? Here are some precautions to keep in mind while you are out and about on foot:

- Just as a burglar looks for an unlocked home that's an easy target, a mugger or rapist looks for potential victims who will offer little or no resistance. Don't appear vulnerable. Walk confidently with your head up and your eyes open. Don't daydream.

- Thwart pickpockets and pursesnatchers by carrying a wallet in a front pants pocket or inside jacket pocket; or by keeping a tight grip on your purse or purse strap. Carry a shoulder bag with the strap going diagonally across your chest; don't let it dangle from your shoulder.

- Carry little cash and only the credit cards you know you'll need. Consider keeping a small amount of cash separate from your purse or wallet as a ready handout to a would-be mugger. If you toss the money on the ground and run the other way, the mugger is likely to go after the cash, not you.

- Carry a loud whistle or noisemaker on your keychain particularly if you will be out alone after dark.

Keep the keychain separate from your purse; hold it in your hand as you walk.

- If you walk or jog, leave the stereo headphones at home. Listening to a tape may make you deaf to an approaching attacker and more vulnerable as a potential victim. Also, avoid dark and narrow places such as alleys, deserted parks, or rows of tall hedges where a criminal could wait in hiding. Whenever possible, jog with a friend or in a well-populated place. Walk on the side of the street facing traffic.

- Try to avoid using automated teller machines after dark.

- If you feel you need added protection, consider a self-defense device such as a personal alarm, chemical spray or stun gun. Not all of these are legal in every state. You operate a *personal electronic alarm* by pulling a pin or pressing a switch. They deliver an earsplitting screech that may startle an assailant long enough for you to get away. *Chemical devices* include tear gas, pepper spray, and dyes that mark an attacker. *Stunners* may stop an attacker by zapping him with electrical current. Call your local police department for information about what is permitted where you live.

- When you are staying at a motel or hotel, keep your door locked, leave valuables locked in a safe at the front desk, and don't leave money or attractive items out in plain sight in your room.

17. DON'T INVITE CAR THEFT

Usually, car thieves strike when the driver is not around, and they hit with alarming frequency. In 1991, 1.6 million vehicles were stolen in the U.S. What can you do to keep your car (and yourself) safe? Ask an expert:

A locked Cadillac will lose out to a Volkswagen with keys in the ignition. As a long-time car thief, I'll always look for keys, first in the ignition, then in the ash tray, visor, glove compartment or under the seat. I don't always carry a tool with me to break into the ignition, and besides, a cop may come by and see some dangling wires. So always take your keys and lock your car.

Packages: I know there's got to be something valuable in that box or bag lying on the backseat of that car. I'm bored, I'm short of money, no one's looking, so I'll just grab a rock, smash the window, take the bag and start walking. What? It was only a sack lunch? Or an old pair of gym shoes? Oh well. No loss, to me. Now you have a cold ride home and an expensive car window bill. So don't advertise. Lock your boxes and bags in the trunk. It was designed to hold things. Use it.

Do yourself a favor and spend about $200 on a security system. In the quiet of night it can and will scare the dickens out of the potential car thief and send him scurrying for cover. I know.

Lowell H., New Mexico

- Before you leave your car, roll up the windows and lock the doors. When you return to your car, have your keys out and ready. Glance in and around your car to see if anything looks suspicious.

- Lock doors routinely while you drive. Do not pick up hitchhikers and do not stop to help stranded motorists; if you see someone who needs help, go to a safe place and call the police.

- Do not place your purse or any valuables in the front passenger seat. A robber can smash the window, grab the purse and disappear in the time it takes to sit through a red light.

- Refuel before your gas gauge reads "empty." Be certain your car is in good repair with all its lights working properly. If you do get stranded, raise the hood and tie a white cloth to the antenna or display a sign saying "Help—Call Police." Stay inside your car and keep it locked. If someone offers to help, crack your window and say, "Call police."

- If your car is bumped from behind under suspicious circumstances, don't get out. Drive slowly to the nearest well-lit, busy area, motioning for the other driver to follow. An aspiring carjacker will flee.

- If you have a garage, drive in head first so your headlights light up the entire space. Using a remote garage door opener when you are still several houses away can scare off a burglar.

- Supply your car with a flashlight, fresh batteries, flares, jumper cables, a fire extinguisher, and a first-aid kit. Consider investing in a car phone if you spend a lot of time behind the wheel.

- Supplemental security devices such as "The Club" that immobilize the steering wheel, lock the brakes, or prevent shifting the transmission are substantial deterrents to auto theft. They should be clearly visible from outside the car.

- Brian C., an inmate doing time in Texas for car theft adds,

  A helpful prevention is to have each individual piece of glass on your auto engraved with the vehicle's identification number. I own and operate a paint and body shop in Houston and had begun to offer just this service to my customers.

- Ask your insurance company whether it offers a discount on your policy if you engrave your car or install an alarm system.

For more information, contact:

Citizens for Auto-theft Responsibility
P.O. Box 3131
Palm Beach, FL 33480
407-478-8990

18. TO SCHOOL AND BEYOND

Schools have grown alarmingly dangerous, particularly where guns and drugs proliferate. Keeping students safe is a preoccupation of teachers and administrators alike, and parental involvement makes a big difference.

- If your children walk to school, get them in the habit of taking a safe, well-traveled route rather than obscure shortcuts.

- Do not send them out with monogrammed clothing or backpacks. A stranger who calls a child by name gains an instant advantage.

- It is unlikely that your child will ever be kidnapped or disappear. However, it may give you peace of mind to take some simple precautions. Many police stations will fingerprint your child and issue an I.D. card with a photograph. Having this on file and keeping current photos at home will speed up the search for a missing child.

- Children should be taught not to hang around aimlessly in public areas or parks. As much as possible, they should remain in groups and stick with an activity or errand.

- Talk to your school's principal and PTA board about safety measures, including the policy for students who leave school with an adult who is not their parent or guardian.

The U.S. Justice Department advises, "Get together with other parents if you find these measures lacking or weak, and work together with school officials and local law enforcement to beef up school security. You won't be sorry!"

- Consider starting a "Block Parent" or "McGruff Safe Home" program in your community. These programs recruit at-home parents, grandparents, and retirees to make their homes available temporarily for lost or frightened children. Volunteers receive special training. A sign is posted in their window to let children know they may go there if they run into trouble.

- McGruff the Crime Dog, the mascot of the National Crime Prevention Council, is an extremely effective "teacher." See the resource list on page 169 for the NCPC's address. Write to them and ask for brochures and other materials for children.

- Ask whether your school teaches the "Fourth R"— relationships. A number of conflict resolution programs are designed to teach kids how to get along.

- Teach your children what to do if they feel threatened:

  1. Run away fast.

  2. Scream loudly.

  3. Go where there are other people.

  4. Tell someone what happened.

19. STAY SAFE AT WORK

I used to steal anything and everything I could conceal, from department stores, grocery stores, drug stores, convenience stores, even men's clothing stores. Once, incredibly, I stole a $200 leather jacket from a fine men's clothier. I still don't know how I did it, but the lustful feeling of power I felt was, at the time, seemingly euphoric.

I should never have gone into a store alone.

Employees speaking to me would have curbed a lot of it.

Shoplifters Anonymous (based on AA's principles) should have been better publicized in my community.

The very first time I was caught, I should have been made to get counseling for the problem.

Ed McD., North Carolina

Crime may strike your place of business from within and without—from employees who steal and from outsiders who shoplift or break in.

Find out if your place of business needs to beef up security by ordering "Curtailing Crime Inside and Out," U.S. Small Business Administration, Management Aid Number CP2, P.O. Box 30, Denver, CO 80201-0030. The cost is $2.

Secure your building and stay alert. Here is what three seasoned prisoners advise:

1. Find out whether your alarm system may be easily thwarted.

    Nearly every store has a sticker . . . that says this place is alarmed. In most cases, you can bypass it. What you do is write down the store's phone number, then go home and call that number. The alarm system goes through the telephone line (to alert the police). If you call the number, the phone inside the store will ring, and as long as the phone is ringing the line is busy and the alarm cannot go out. So you go to the back of the store and kick the door in or enter through a window. And it's all yours.

Luke S., New Mexico

2. Discourage drop-ins.

Try checking all the air ducts even on top of your business. A lot of burglars I have known weigh 150 pounds or less, and all they need is room enough for their head. Where the head fits, so will the rest of them. I've even known guys to bring a small hatchet to knock a hole in the roof of a place and drop in from the ceiling. Also check to see whether adjacent buildings might be used (to gain entry) instead of a ladder.

Andy N., Florida

3. Check out everyone who writes a check.

I bounced about $3,000 in checks and stole others' personal checks, forged and cashed them. . . . I went to stores, bought items legitimately and purposely started friendly conversations. I would introduce myself as whomever the stolen checks belonged to. I'd go back to the store often, buy small items, and become easily recognized by name. Once I had established a rapport, I'd buy a large number of expensive items, forge the check and was rarely asked for an I.D.

Keith B., Oklahoma

- Employees should speak directly to everyone who enters a shop or store. Law-abiding customers welcome the attention; a shoplifter does not. Employees also need to watch for shoppers who wander aimlessly, who arrive in groups which then split up, or who tote large bags or wear loose clothing that could conceal stolen items.

• Plan a seminar on crime prevention for your company or organization. Through its 50-plus regional offices, Citizens Against Crime presents programs free of charge to businesses and community groups. They discuss ways to avoid, escape or survive robbery, assault, rape and burglary. To find out more, call 1-800-466-5566.

• You can bank on it. . . . If you work in a bank, you may be especially vulnerable to a robbery attempt. Two imprisoned bank robbers tell what would have deterred them:

If there was a guard inside each bank, I would not have robbed even one. The physical presence of any type of guard tells you they are aware of the possibility of a robbery and that they have some sort of structure to prevent it.

Charles M., California

I only initiated the crime if there were female employees in the bank (because) a female teller would be more likely to meet the demand. . . . The time of day I chose was 12 noon while most of the work force was having lunch. So, keep male and female tellers working together. A second deterrent is a plexiglass or bar-type partition above the teller windows. When I entered a bank and there were partitions above and between myself and the tellers, I left. The partition gives the perpetrator far less control of the situation.

Bud G., Virginia

20. LET PRISONERS CONTRIBUTE TO BETTER COMMUNITIES

If no criminal ever set foot in your neighborhood, you would feel perfectly confident about staying safe from crime. But this is not a perfect world. The fact is, even when criminals are caught, convicted, and sent to prison, most of them will reenter their communities one day. More and more programs are being designed to help these men and women lead productive and law-abiding lives. Sometimes, the biggest obstacle they face is community opposition—those who say "not in my backyard" to halfway houses or group homes. Yet some communities are learning to welcome former inmates with creative acceptance and appropriate safeguards.

A retired sheriff in Omaha was confined to a wheelchair by severe emphysema. His house needed repairs. He couldn't afford to pay for them and certainly couldn't do the work himself. In cooperation with the Omaha Correctional Center Work Release Unit, Prison Fellowship and two local churches arranged for the furlough of five trustworthy prisoners, who then built a new roof over the sheriff's leaky garage, painted the house, fixed the porch, and installed a new rain gutter. The market value of the work was $8,500. The prisoners and church volunteers provided free labor, while PF and local donations paid for supplies. The sheriff paid with a heartfelt "Thank you." In 1992, 130 prisoners and 133 churches participated in 25

Prison Fellowship programs nationwide like this one, known as Community Service Projects.

In Ohio, the MonDay Program (named for Montgomery County and Dayton) places convicted residents in volunteer community service jobs. In this way, the men and women serving time gain self-esteem and learn to view the community from a caring, giving perspective.

1. Residents plant and mulch trees and do minor maintenance for the County Park District.

2. At a local nursing home, they visit with senior citizens and help with recreational activities and personal grooming (such as manicures).

3. At the Kettering Developmental Center for Handicapped Children, MonDay volunteers assist with a variety of activities.

4. Residents present panel discussions on topics such as drugs and alcoholism at local schools, churches, and community groups.

5. They sort and label merchandise at Salvation Army stores, provide child care, and assist with clerical tasks.

IF YOU ARE A VICTIM

A conversation with the survivors (relatives) of my murder victim . . . brought me to grips with my own culpability and personal feelings of guilt. I asked them what I could do now. They said, "Reach out to the victims. There are a lot of questions they want answered that the district attorney, the defense attorney, can't answer—only you can answer."

Craig S., California

21. REHEARSE YOUR RESPONSE

When you drive, knowing alternate routes can relieve anxiety in case of a roadblock or detour. The same holds true with crime. If you take time now to review your strengths, strategies, and what you've learned so far about crime and criminals, you have a better chance of keeping some control if you become a crime victim.

- Practice being alert. If you are tuned in to your surroundings, you will be more likely to avoid places where a crime might occur and you will see trouble coming. Size up the places where you ordinarily walk and drive, and keep observing the people and cars around you.

- Stay calm. If you do not plan ahead, you are more likely to be gripped by paralyzing fear at the split second you realize you're being threatened. During that first moment, the criminal is apt to be experiencing extreme fear and agitation as well. Remaining as panic free as possible may keep you focused and alert for an opportunity to escape, resist, cry for help, and to observe important details about your assailant.

- Don't enrage. If the situation affords a chance to talk to your assailant, decide ahead of time to swallow your rage. If you view him as a person, not an object, you make it harder for him to depersonalize you.

Candace L. Walters, counselor and author, says, "Attempt to engage your attacker in conversation; tell him about your family, ask about his. Try to get him to see you as someone's sister, daughter, or mother, and ask how he would feel if his relative was raped."

- Draw on your strengths. Have you taken a self-defense course or assertiveness training? Do you carry a whistle or a defensive spray? Imagine using a tactic against an assailant. Plan where you would keep items for self-defense and time how quickly you could grab them. If you feel uncomfortable about a particular form of self-defense, then do not rely on it or get further instruction about how to use it.

"A group of convicted rapists was asked what their victims could have done to prevent the attack. The overwhelming response was to make them see her as a real person with real feelings and understand how damaging the assault would be for her. When they could not depersonalize the woman and distance themselves emotionally from her suffering, they did not rape" (Candace L. Walters, *Invisible Wounds: Becoming Streetwise about Sexual Assault,* [Portland, OR: Multnomah, reprinted 1992], 130-31).

I'm in prison for rape. If as a child I had been told . . . that crime does really hurt people I doubt I'd have committed this crime. I was 15 years old at the time. I'm now 33, and I see now that my crime against this person has hurt her all her life.

John L., Virginia

91

22. RESIST OR SUBMIT?

Advance preparation may help you size up a criminal encounter, but it cannot dictate exactly how you should respond. Deciding to resist, flee, or submit to an assailant's demands may be the most difficult and harrowing choice of your life. Here is what you should keep in mind:

At home:

- If you hear someone break into your home at night, stay put! Lock your bedroom door and quietly call the police. If a thief is in your bedroom, pretend to stay asleep until he leaves.

- If you return home to evidence of a break-in, such as a broken window or a door swinging open, do not go inside. Call police from a neighbor's home or a pay phone.

- Do not let a stranger enter your home. If someone needs to make a call, volunteer to make the call yourself or hand the person your cordless phone.

On the street:

- It bears repeating: never pick up a hitchhiker—ever.

- Do not drive or walk home if you suspect someone is following you. Head for a well-lit shop, gas station, police station, or other place where people are present.

- If the person who assaults you has a gun or a knife and says you are being robbed, do not resist. Quickly determine what he wants: your money, jewelry, car, or other possessions. Relinquish them at once while you memorize how the assailant looks.

- If the assailant threatens to kidnap, rape, or otherwise harm you, experts advise screaming or yelling something besides "Help." Yell "I'm being hurt" or "call police" or even "fire," and run away. If that is not possible, stall for time and try reasoning with the attacker. Some victims have escaped harm by making themselves vomit or urinate, or by feigning mental illness. Above all, trust your instincts.

- If you feel confident about your ability to resist an unarmed attacker, do not "fight fair." Use any means possible to disable an assailant including gouging his eyes, kicking his groin, jabbing his throat, scratching and biting. If you fight, stay mad not scared!

> "Anytime you are forced to have sexual contact against your will it is sexual assault. The term rape refers specifically to sexual intercourse. Whether or not you know your assailant, whether or not you struggle physically, there is still a difference between giving consent and submitting out of fear. . . . If you are threatened with violence and submit to a sexual act out of fear for your life or safety, you have not consented. You have been raped" ("Sexual Assault: It Could Happen to You," Victim Assistance Network, Alexandria, VA).

23. MEMORIZE DETAILS

Victims can help fight crime by accurately remembering details. According to the National Crime Prevention Council, "If victims are good witnesses they convict offenders. That can help keep criminals away from all of us." After you have been assaulted, write down everything you can remember about the crime. Here are guidelines adapted from police department crime-prevention materials:

What did the suspect look like?

1. Sex—male or female.

2. Race, complexion—light, medium, dark.

3. Age—approximate.

4. Height—estimate in two-inch blocks (between 5'8"and 5'10") or compare to door, shelves, etc.

5. Weight—estimate in blocks of ten pounds (130 to 140).

6. Build—large, small, stocky, thin, any tattoos or scars.

7. Eyes, nose, ears—glasses, unusual or prominent features.

8. Hair—color, thick or thin, balding or full; beard or mustache.

9. Clothing—start at the top and work down.

10. Voice—accent, any verbal clues of identity.

Example: Male, white, fair complexion, approximately 25 years old, between 5'7" and 5'9", 140 to 150 pounds. Slender build. Blue eyes, bushy eyebrows, gold stud in left earlobe. Blond hair, thin, straight; no facial hair. Wearing black turtleneck, denim jacket, jeans, running shoes.

What did the vehicle look like?

1. Color.

2. Make and year—estimate late model or old.

3. Body type—sedan, convertible, minivan.

4. License number—specify state.

5. Distinguishing marks—dents or damage; bumper stickers or roof rack.

6. Direction of travel—what street is it on, which cross street is it approaching?

7. Number of people in the car and what they look like.

Example: White Toyota Corolla, late model, two-door sedan. Pennsylvania license plate. Bent rear bumper. Traveling south on Oak Street approaching Main. Two males, black, 18 to 20 years old, wearing sweatshirts.

24. REPORT VIOLENT CRIME

As soon as possible after your encounter with a violent criminal, get to a safe place and call the police. Give them a head start on finding and arresting a person who may endanger others. Here is what you may expect:

- When you call the police, the patrol car nearest you will be dispatched to the scene.

- While you are waiting for the officer to arrive, leave everything exactly as it is. Do not clean up after a burglary, or change clothes or bathe after reporting a rape, because you may destroy crucial evidence that could lead to an arrest. Do not discuss the crime with other witnesses. Make individual notes about what happened.

- The officer will question you about what happened and will note all the descriptive details you can recall. Answer factually; do not guess or exaggerate.

- Later, the officer may ask you to come to the station and try to identify your assailant from photographs, or you may assist police artists as they compile a sketch of the criminal.

- If a suspect is arrested, you may be required to appear in court to identify your assailant.

You will be considered a witness for the state. As criminal proceedings move forward, you may have difficulty finding out about the case. It comes as a surprise to many crime victims that they do not really have an official "place" in the criminal justice system. The current system views crime as injuring the state, not an individual or a community. In order to recover your financial loss, you need to get in touch with a victim compensation program in your state or file suit in civil court.

• Don't underestimate the trauma of crime. Call a friend to be with you after it occurs, and take someone along with you when you go to court. Consider talking with a counselor or therapist.

"When William the Conquerer became king of England, he took title to all land. He then portioned it out to his supporters and to the church. He and his descendants asserted increasing control over the process by which crimes and other judicial matters were disposed of. . . . Criminal punishments were no longer viewed primarily as ways of restoring the victims of crime, but instead as a means of redressing 'injury' to the king.

"As a result, the victim had no remedy. The criminal proceeding generated fines for the king. . . . The punishment of crime had become the province of the state. Recovery by the victim was a private matter to be settled in the civil courts" (Daniel W. Van Ness, *Crime and its Victims* [Downers Grove, IL: InterVarsity Press, 1986], 66-67).

This view of crime, rooted in the Middle Ages, is essentially the same theory that guides criminal justice today, even though some improvements have come about in recent years. It's important to keep in mind that the state, not an individual, is the *legal* victim. When you feel left out or ignored by officials in the criminal justice system, it isn't that they personally don't value you; rather, the system needs you only to the extent that you can be helpful as a witness.

25. IF YOUR CHILD IS A VICTIM

It's a parent's worst nightmare: discovering evidence of child abuse or molestation. The National Crime Prevention Council offers these suggestions:

- Believe your child. Children rarely lie about sexual abuse.

- Affirm your child for telling you and convey your support. A child's greatest fear is that he or she is to blame. It is essential to help undo this sense of self-blame.

- Do your best to remain calm and temper your own reaction, recognizing that your perspective sends important signals to your child. Try not to convey your horror about the abuse.

- Report the suspected incident to a social services agency or the police.

- Seek out a specialized agency to evaluate your child—a hospital program, child welfare agency, or community mental health group.

- Be aware of physical symptoms that may indicate abuse even if your child isn't talking about it. These include extreme changes in behavior such as loss of appetite; nightmares or disturbed sleep patterns; regression to infantile behavior such as bedwetting or thumb sucking; bleeding, pain, itching, or swelling of genitals; unusual interest in or knowledge of sexual matters; fear of a person or an intense dislike of being left at a certain place or with a certain person.

- Talk with other parents whose children may be affected to find out if they are detecting similar symptoms or complaints.

- Taking action promptly is critical because if you do nothing, more children will be at risk.

- Do not blame yourself. Many individuals who molest children work and volunteer in places where they have access to children. The vast majority of abuse occurs where the child knows and trusts the adult or juvenile.

For more information, contact:

National Council on Child Abuse and Family Violence
1155 Connecticut Ave., N.W. Suite 400
Washington, D.C. 20036
Telephone 202-429-6695

National Family Violence Help Line: 1-800-222-2000

Childhelp USA's National Child Abuse Hotline:
1-800-422-4453 (1-800-4-A-CHILD)

I am guilty of sexually abusing my own daughter and was also once a victim of abuse myself. . . . I can only remember bits and pieces of my childhood abuse, although I have been working hard to recall it. I can remember being physically abused by a stepfather and homosexually abused by older boys who were children of a friend of the family. I believe it has caused me a lot of problems in my life, but I don't believe it can be used as an excuse for what I did.

My daughter was 12 at the time and today at the age of 16 there is still the pain of what I did to her. I have a picture of her on my wall and when I look at her eyes I see this pain and the confusion of not understanding what she did to cause this bad thing to happen to her. I can only hope that someday she will realize that what happened to her wasn't her fault, but only the fault of a father's lust, selfishness and insensitivity.

Mark S., Texas

26. GET VICTIM ASSISTANCE

Since 1980, victim assistance programs have flourished, thanks largely to the efforts of the National Organization for Victim Assistance (NOVA). This group is in contact with as many as 10,000 victims each year, referring most of them to services near their own communities. NOVA also supports legislation designed to protect the rights of victims, and it assists professionals and volunteers who help victims. If you are a victim, why do you need assistance and what do you need?

- You will experience intense emotions, including shock, disorientation, fear, and anger. Worst, according to experts, are ongoing, anxious feelings of violation and vulnerability. Victim assistance programs offer crisis intervention, short-term counseling, and long-term therapy. They will provide someone to meet with you and talk with you, helping you cope with devastating feelings.

- You are thrust into the midst of a confusing process of police work and court proceedings, and you may feel neglected and forgotten. Victim assistance organizations can assist you in filing insurance forms, requesting compensation, and keeping informed about what is happening to your assailant through the process of trial, sentencing, and punishment. Practical help may be offered, such as transportation, child care, and someone to accompany you during difficult appearances in court.

• For referral to your nearest victim assistance program, call INFOLINK, a service of the National Victim Center, at 1-800-FYI-CALL.

Rights for Victims and Witnesses

1. To be treated with dignity and compassion.

2. To receive protection from intimidation and harm.

3. To be informed about the criminal justice process.

4. To receive legal counsel.

5. To get your money back or have hospital bills paid.

6. To have your property and employment preserved.

7. To be provided due process in criminal court proceedings.

For more information, contact:

National Organization for Victim Assistance (NOVA)
1757 Park Road, N.W.
Washington, D.C., 20010
202-232-6682

Neighbors Who Care
P.O. Box 17500
Washington, D.C. 20041
703-904-7311

Anyone can provide emotional first aid to a victim through these simple statements:
"I'm sorry it happened."
"I'll be with you through this."
"You have been wronged."

27. WHAT DO YOU REALLY WANT THE COURTS TO DO?

A drunk driver struck Sherry Kuehl's car on an interstate highway, leaving her with a shattered pelvis. She spent two months in traction and more than a year relearning how to walk. The drunk driver was a young man named Steven—a Vietnam vet with a history of brain seizures. Unable to make bail, he spent three months in jail awaiting sentencing.

Sherry filled out a victim impact statement and was asked to recommend a punishment for Steven. She learned more about him, and she began working to keep him from going to prison. Sherry had never heard of alternative sentencing, but that's what she wanted: four years of probation, treatment for substance abuse, proper medical attention for his brain disorder, and 1,296 volunteer hours on an orthopedic ward—the same number of hours Sherry had spent in the hospital.

Sherry was amazed when the judge followed her recommendations to the letter. For four years after the accident, Sherry heard from Steven, who fulfilled his community service sentence by working in a local nursing home. In his letters Steven repeatedly wrote, "Thank you for giving me a second chance at life" (Adapted from Deborah Kinnaird and Evelyn Bence, "When Justice Walks In," *Jubilee*, September 1991, 6).

Some criminal offenders need to be locked up to prevent them from injuring more victims. Many others can benefit from alternatives to prison. These alternatives are sometimes called "intermediate" or "reparative" sanctions. They are part of an approach to criminal justice that focuses on healing the wounds caused by crime—wounds to individuals, communities, and wounds the offender has brought upon himself.

If you are a crime victim, you may hold sway over how your assailant is treated in court, just as Sherry Kuehl did. Here are some points about reparative sanctions to keep in mind as you consider what to do next:

- Sending a non-violent offender to prison locks him into a system where positive change rarely happens.

- In prison, offenders have scant opportunity to face up to the harm they've caused their victims. Instead, studies show convicts tend to deny personal responsibility, blaming their actions on factors outside their control; they deny hurting anyone and they depersonalize their victim; they tend to focus on the perceived unfairness of their accusers, the police, and the courts.

- In contrast, reparative sanctions emphasize the offender's personal responsibility for the hurt he or she has caused. They also provide a way for offenders to pay back victims, either directly or symbolically.

- Examples of reparative sanctions are detailed on pages 153–54.

Victims in Quincy, Massachusetts, receive payment directly from the criminals who robbed or burglarized them, thanks to the Community Service Program (CSP). The program, which started in 1975 and was first called Earn-It, matches convicted offenders with temporary minimum-wage jobs. Two-thirds of their earnings go toward restitution, and they may keep the rest. CSP is run by the Probation Department of Quincy District Court, in cooperation with local businesses and the Chamber of Commerce. Offenders must qualify for the program.

28. PARTICIPATE IN A VORP

The hardest part of my, thus far, fourteen years isn't the prison's racial riots and violence. The hardest part was facing my victim's survivors and listening to how their lives were impacted. The hardest part was facing my own loving family and realizing . . . the public scorn they have experienced. The hardest part was coming to grips with my own culpability and looking at myself in the mirror, admitting my guilt, and humbling myself on my knees in prayer.

Craig S., California

Craig F. Stevenson, the prisoner quoted here, is serving a life term for murder. When he was incarcerated in Vacaville, California, he and other inmates became involved in a growing movement to bring victims face to face with prisoners. The Vacaville inmates gather weekly, along with representatives from victims' groups such as Mothers Against Drunk Driving. They emphasize accepting responsibility for criminal actions and recovering from destructive behavior patterns.

Most crime victims never confront their assailants again, except perhaps in an impersonal court room. Often, profoundly troubling questions go unanswered: "Why did he victimize me?" "Had he been watching our home or stalking us?" "Does he have any idea how devastated we feel?"

In more than one hundred communities nationwide, meetings between victims and offenders are being arranged by a variety of locally based Victim-Offender Reconciliation Programs (VORPs). The meetings are run in cooperation with the courts as a recognized component of the criminal justice system. Organizers do not expect participants to feel all their hurt and rage melt away instantly—"most VORP cases at best plant tiny seeds of restoration that take root in the process of reparation and the experience of having a voice in the aftermath of crime," according to a Justice Fellowship research monograph. What happens when victim and offender meet? The process is described by Ron Claassen, director of the Center for Conflict Studies and Peacemaking, Fresno Pacific College, Fresno, CA, and a leader in developing VORPs:

- The case is screened by a VORP coordinator, then passed on to a volunteer mediator. A staff member or the mediator meets separately with offender and victim. Approximately half of the cases referred for VORP actually result in a meeting.

- The meeting is convened with the mediator present. There are three agenda items:

  1. *Recognizing the injustice.* The facts of the offense are reviewed. What did the offender do, and why? What was the victim's experience and subsequent feelings?

  2. *Restoring equity.* What can the offender do to make things as right as possible, recognizing that there is no way to undo the offense? Paying the victim back is one way to restore some equity.

  3. *Making clear agreements.* Most victims want to be assured that the offender will not strike again. A

detailed, written agreement about what the offender will do is the result of almost every VORP meeting.

- After the meeting ends, the mediator writes a report and an evaluation. The VORP coordinator monitors the case, checking with the victim or the referring agency until restitution is made. If problems arise, either the coordinator or mediator helps to renegotiate the agreement.

- Even if you cannot participate in a formal VORP meeting, you may have an unexpected opportunity to reconcile with an offender. A prisoner from Minnesota writes,

My crimes range from burglary, theft, selling of drugs, using drugs, selling stolen property, etc. I've been involved in these activities since a very young age, and I'm tired of it all. I just want to live a clean, healthy life. . . . I've already started this process by accepting Jesus Christ into my life and then by going directly to the last people whom I attempted to burglarize and ask them for their forgiveness and let them know that I truly am sorry for what I had done to them. Well, they responded and much to my amazement they accepted and we are now Christian friends. We have a long ways to go, but we know that Christ is on our side, and through him I will be set free from my life of a criminal, drug user and a very lonely person.

Martin A., Minnesota

For more information contact:

U.S. Association for Victim-Offender Mediation
PACT Institute of Justice
254 S. Morgan Boulevard
Valparaiso, Indiana 46383
219-462-1127

Center for Conflict Studies and Peacemaking
Fresno Pacific College
1717 S. Chestnut Ave.
Fresno, CA 93702

"The mediation process helps victims reduce their anger, frustration and fear and compensates them for their losses. Offenders, meanwhile, are held accountable for their behavior and have the chance to make amends. . . . Although it is not appropriate in all cases, victim-offender mediation is an effective criminal justice tool that vividly expresses the principles of restorative justice" (Mark S. Umbreit, Ph.D., Center for Victim Offender Mediation, "Having Offenders Meet with their Victims Offers Benefits for Both Parties", *Corrections Today*, July 1991, 166).

CHANGING LIVES

I can't pinpoint when or how I crossed the point of no return. Any criminal will ultimately cross that line which, for most of us, leaves only the brick wall of death or arrest. There is that point when nobody, including yourself, can stop you. By this time you've either run off those who really care about you or, worse, drug them down with you.

Hank D., California

29. KEEP TEENAGERS OCCUPIED

Young people whose energies are channeled in positive directions are less likely to resort to delinquent behavior. Travis Hirschi, in his book *Causes of Delinquency*, identifies several traits that keep kids crime free: being committed to accomplishing a goal, getting involved in activities such as sports or music, and learning respect for parents and others in authority.

Not every child is lucky enough to have parents and others in his or her life to model and teach these traits. When that happens, young people turn to their peers for guidance and approval, often with disastrous consequences. They become involved in crime or they become victims. The National Crime Prevention Council estimates there are more than 2000 violent crimes committed by strangers against teenagers every day.

- If you are a parent, search out ways to engage teens in activities they enjoy and that challenge them physically, spiritually, emotionally, or intellectually.

- Model goal-setting yourself and help your children set realistic, meaningful goals.

- Get teenagers involved in mentoring or tutoring programs for at-risk youth.

A well-defined purpose in life would have prevented me from breaking the law. So many young people have no purpose, no meaning, and no direction. It has been said that if you don't stand for something, you'll fall for anything.

Drugs have given people a false purpose in life. It gave me a way to escape the realities of life and also a means to support my habit. Alcohol and drugs are being consumed at an all-time high. They're killing more and more people every day. They're causing prisons to be overcrowded, hospitals and treatment centers to be filled, and innocent people to be hurt.

Drugs are destroying our families and becoming the only hope that some people have. I still think drugs are only a symptom of a much larger problem. . . . Until we begin to nurture, mold, guide and direct our young people in a positive way, things will just get worse. Drugs and alcohol will continue to grow in popularity and control the minds and lives of millions.

Richard F., Michigan

30. LET KIDS KNOW WHAT CRIME IS REALLY LIKE

It is not unusual for kids to hold a view of crime and criminals that is unrealistically glamorous and exciting. Fed by cartoons, movies, and relentless portrayals of cops and killers on television, they may have no clue about the chilling realities of a life of crime or time spent behind bars.

Through schools and other community programs, inmates are telling their stories as a counterweight to popular media myths. Perhaps a program is available near you; your state's Department of Corrections can tell you what inmates are doing to get the word out:

- "The Choice is Yours" was developed by death-row inmate Roger Keith Coleman, who was executed for the murder of his sister-in-law. It began as an open letter to middle-school counselors, and it "describes a typical day on death row and warns against committing a crime," Coleman wrote. He went on to describe what happened:

  In October of 1982 I began sending copies of TCIY to every juvenile judge and junior and senior high school counseling department in the state, many of whom used it. Since the program began, I've received letters from more than 500 young people, many of whom thought prison was a bed of roses before reading my letter. . . . Kids from ages 9 to 19 have written me. They come to me with problems such as peer pressure to drink, take drugs, running away, fighting, dropping out of school and many other problems facing today's youth. . . . I expected parents to object to their children writing to a death row prisoner, but it's been just the opposite. A lot of kids have told me that their parents have encouraged them to write me (sort of to get it straight from the horse's mouth!).

On two occasions parents have brought their kids here to see me so I could talk to them face to face about prison life.

Since it started, The Choice is Yours has been used at federal Job Corps centers and elsewhere in an effort to reach young people.

- At the Bland Correctional Center in Bland, Virginia, inmates speak to school children and church groups through Programs Assisting Youth (PAY). In its first three years, the prisoners reached some 3000 children with an anti-drug, anti-crime message. The program assists the prisoners as well: one wrote that because of PAY, he has "had a chance to read an enormous amount of material concerning schools, parents, and kids."

- In Louisiana, a recognized Toastmasters chapter took shape several years ago at the Phelps Correctional Center. Prisoners who participated in it developed a Drug and Alcohol Awareness Program available to schools, churches and youth groups throughout southwest Louisiana. The seminars covered the physical and mental effects of drugs and alcohol, how to say no, and how to cope with peer pressure. Today, the seminar material is available on videotape for outside groups.

People have to realize how much gets taken away from them when they do crimes and get caught. . . . My freedom was an everyday, no-problem thing. It was there and I was in it. Now that it is gone and I know how much it means to me, I never want to gamble with my freedom again. . . . In prison you are humiliated every day, never get to make your own decisions, like when you want to get out of bed or go and eat and when to go to sleep. You only see your family for two hours a week. People really need to feel how good freedom is and appreciate it.

Allen T., Texas

31. HELP PARENTS LEARN BETTER SKILLS

This is what my childhood was like for me. I was told all the time I was growing up that I was no-good and would never amount to anything. I was beaten with a razor strap every time my dad got mad, which was almost every day of the week. . . . I wasn't allowed to have any friends come over and for my own reasons I never made any friends. I tell you this, my life before coming to prison (wasn't) much different. I am still living my life as a loner.

Joe W., Michigan

Letters from prisoners confirm a strong link between their childhood experiences and later criminal behavior. More than one-fifth of the inmates who wrote to us cited "parental guidance" as a factor that could have stopped them from crime. In many cases, these men and women report suffering severe abuse or neglect. At the same time, many others noted their own role in a cycle of escalating family frustration and violence. "I wouldn't listen to them," one inmate wrote. A hostile home life poorly equips children for the stresses they meet later at school or on the street, and it drives them into a different circle of influence: a peer group that may pressure them relentlessly into making bad choices.

It's true that many people from severely disadvantaged backgrounds succeed and lead positive, productive, law-abiding lives. And kids raised in loving, intact families sometimes make bad choices. Nevertheless, the family is more and more recognized as a critically important factor in shaping attitudes and behaviors beginning in early childhood. At one time or another, all parents—from all walks of life and every strata of income—need support and training.

- Your experience as a parent could be invaluable to other parents. Find out if classes in parenting are held at your community center, local YMCA, or school system's continuing education department. See if they need your help.

- Ask if your local high school or community college offers a parenting curriculum or includes these sorts of skills in related classes. Consider forming a parents' committee to research available materials and introduce them to your school.

- Numerous books about parenting are available for use with small groups or larger adult education classes at your church. Propose a class on a parenting topic such as building character at home. Then advertise it locally to attract others who may want guidance.

- It's never too late. In the District of Columbia, a corrections department program called Concerned Fathers teaches practical parenting skills to imprisoned men and encourages them to take an active role in their children's lives. As a result, prison officials hope these men will have stronger family ties when they are released and that they can successfully steer their own youngsters away from criminal behavior.

"I believe that parent training ought to be a mandatory course in every high school in our nation. This form of teaching is not outside our educational tradition. We used to teach home economics. Every girl in the nation learned to sew and cook. Today we need to teach every girl and boy how to parent, how to love and care for children, how to discipline them, how to provide for their developmental needs. . . . Most of us become parents. Few of us are prepared for the job" (*Deadly Consequences*, 157).

32. TEACH SOMEONE TO READ

The ability to read is more than just a skill people need to get through school and get a job. It is a key source of self-esteem and accomplishment. Often, school dropouts give up on their studies because they feel like failures. They can't keep up because they cannot read. Even though many are very intelligent, they are treated as if they are not.

Being illiterate does not mean a person will turn to crime, yet research shows many who turn to crime cannot read. A report in *Corrections Compendium* notes, "No matter which statistics are used, a significant link between illiteracy and incarceration emerges from the figures" (Dec. 1991, p. 5). As many as three-quarters of prisoners cannot read well enough to follow directions on a prescription or to answer a help-wanted ad after they are released.

- Volunteer with a literacy program. Your school system or local government may have a program that trains and uses volunteers.

- Be honest about whom you could best help. There are all types who need and want help: students who are doing poorly in school, dropouts who want to obtain a high school equivalency degree, new foreign immigrants, older adults who have gotten by without reading for years and want to enrich their lives.

- For more information about literacy training and volunteer opportunities, contact Laubach Literacy International, Box 131, Syracuse, NY 13210, 315-422-9121 or Literacy Volunteers of America, 5795 Widewaters Parkway, Syracuse, NY 13214, 315-445-8000.

In Arizona, a study showed that approximately 60 percent of prison inmates read below a sixth-grade level. In response, an unusual partnership in literacy training took shape between an adult probation department and a local school district. Beginning in 1987, the Arizona Supreme Court purchased an IBM literacy program called PALS (Principles of Alphabet Literacy Systems). Literacy laboratories were established statewide, and agencies wanting to use the program had to agree to give individuals on probation first priority.

One program is run by the Maricopa County Adult Probation Department and the Mesa Unified Public Schools' division of community education. The probation department paid for a program coordinator, supplied the space, insurance, and office supplies. The schools offered six part-time teachers, support staff, educational equipment and supplies. In its first two years of operation, the center provided services to more than 1,000 people, 60 percent of whom were on probation" (Adapted from Paul O'Connell and Jacquelyn M. Power, "Establishing Literacy Programs in Community Corrections," American Probation and Parole Association, *APPA Perspectives,* Fall 1992, 6).

33. KEEP YOUR WORK-PLACE DRUG FREE

- If you see evidence of drug or alcohol abuse by a co-worker or employee, don't delay. Address the problem directly by talking with a supervisor. The employee not only poses a risk to himself or herself and to co-workers, but also to family members.

- Organize a company-wide education program about how alcoholics and drug abusers can be helped in your community—and what the consequences can be if the problem is ignored.

- Seek guidance from a mental health or substance abuse professional about getting the person into treatment. Make certain your health benefits cover treatment programs.

I was not strong enough to stay away from drugs myself, even though I was clever enough to convince most people that I didn't have a problem. I knew that my continued drug use would eventually get me to prison. . . .

The problem is that for someone like myself, by the time crimes have to be committed to support our habits, we have already lost the means to save ourselves. We have a marriage that is falling apart. Most likely we have run out of insurance benefits, and no way are we going to spend our cash on drug rehab.

I can only blame myself for committing my crimes while trying to support my addiction. There was a point when friends and loved ones tried to help, but I would not listen. When I was totally out of control, they were tired of trying to help a "lost cause," and of course it was too late anyway.

Early detection of a behavioral problem while I was still employed may have saved me, as my employer then had a good benefits package which included substance abuse treatment and prevention.

If assistance and counseling are not available upon my release from prison, there is a very good possibility that I will return. Revolving door is not just a cliche in this state, it's a reality. Without an overriding incentive to remain free from drugs, I fear that I may not be able to remain free of prison.

John C., Arizona

34. BE A MENTOR

I'm a 27-year-old black male doing time in prison for larceny from a person. I was 18 years old at the time. Staying at the City Rescue Mission. Nowhere to go and very low self-esteem. I'm in for my first adult felony. I pretended to have a gun and told an older man to hand over his money, which was only $3.84.

I'm from a very small town . . . which offers little or nothing in the way of programs that deal with building young people's self-esteem, showing them positive ways to be successful in life, and helping them to find jobs. If we can find a program that deals with these three problems and find people willing to give it a chance, we will see success. We need more people who care.

Michael S., Michigan

Mentoring programs are based on the idea that a caring adult can make a difference in the life of one troubled or at-risk young person simply by listening, befriending, guiding, and inspiring. Perhaps the best known national mentoring organization is Big Brothers/Big Sisters of America, based in Philadelphia.

If you volunteer to become a Big Brother or Big Sister, you are carefully evaluated and matched with a school-aged child who, in most cases, lives in a single-parent family. The mentoring relationship lasts at least one year. During that time, you meet with your Little Brother or Sister once a week, listening to the child's concerns, going on special outings, or just spending time together.

126

Specific goals for the child are set, and a caseworker is available to answer questions or troubleshoot difficulties.

- Mentoring works. A recent Harris Poll surveyed 400 mentored high school students and 400 mentors nationwide. Of the students, 73 percent said their mentors helped them raise their goals and expectations, 87 percent went to college after graduating or planned to attend college within one year of graduating, and 59 percent saw their grades go up. Mentors benefited as well: 92 percent said they enjoyed the experience and 86 percent said they would be a mentor again.

- There's room for more mentors. More than 15 million children are growing up in one-parent families, according to Big Brothers/Big Sisters of America. Not all of these children need mentors, because some have extended families or other sources of support. Yet an estimated one-fifth of them need more help than one parent alone can provide. Thousands of children are waiting to be placed with mentors, who may be young, old, married, single, and from any ethnic and socioeconomic group.

- Opportunities to help go beyond one-to-one mentoring. Volunteers are needed in leadership roles with local Big Brother/Big Sister agencies and similar groups. Financial assistance, in-kind services, and recruiting are among the needs volunteers can fill.

For information about mentoring opportunities nationwide, write to:

> One to One Partnership, Inc.
> 2801 M Street, N.W.
> Washington, D.C. 20007
> 202-338-3844

> Big Brothers/Big Sisters of America
> 230 N. Thirteenth Street
> Philadelphia, PA 19107-1510
> 215-567-7000

> *Caring people out there (need to) see you as a person who is headed for trouble (and) take time to talk with you or work with you in solving problems. Sure, there are professional counselors who are qualified to do this type of work, but that is not enough. Family, school teachers, and co-workers (could) give encouragement. I really do believe if I had had more encouragement and more concern about my future, the thought of crime would not have even crossed my mind.*

> Pat G., Mississippi

35. TAKE SOME HEAT

People who work on the receiving end of a crisis hotline can play a crucial role in crime prevention. Hotlines are there for all sorts of difficulties—some offer a safety valve for people who feel so hostile, frustrated, or threatened that they contemplate committing a crime or harming themselves. Hotlines are also available for latchkey children, victims of rape or domestic violence, potential child abusers, or those who want to know how to end their dependence on drugs or alcohol.

- Lend an ear. Most hotlines are staffed at least in part by volunteers—members of the community who care about changing lives and have some time available. The programs will provide training and supervision.

- To find out about opportunities near you, check your Yellow Pages under Crisis Intervention Service or Social Service Organizations.

I am a 21-year-old white male. I feel that I have gotten in trouble all my life from hanging around the wrong crowd. Don't take me wrong; I'm not saying I'm an angel—if that was true I wouldn't be here. But to get to the point, I have always had trouble saying "no" to people, and after I broke the law I'd feel bad. I'm in here for receiving stolen property, and I feel if I could have called somebody I wouldn't have done my crime. All I needed was a single person to talk me out of it.

Dave K., Michigan

129

36. HELP SEX OFFENDERS FIND HELP

I am in prison on a sexual charge. I was molested as a youth and became very sexually active at the age of 13. I got caught several times by parents that didn't care enough to press charges, mostly they told me to stay away from their children and that was the end of it, as far as they were concerned. Between the ages of 16 and 30 I was active but never got caught. I was 30 the first time I . . . tried to get help. I was not taken seriously. The most important thing I can say is, take people seriously when they ask for help.

Michael C., Florida

People who suffer sexual abuse when they are children experience an array of difficulties as they grow older. Research convincingly shows many of these victims become sex offenders, repeating the very crimes that distorted their ability to relate to others.

Between 1988 and 1990, the number of sex offenders imprisoned in the United States grew by almost 48 percent. Arrests for sex offenses other than forcible rape totalled 108,000 in 1991. In response, more than 2000 treatment programs have been established nationwide. Treatments including therapy, anger management, support groups, medication, and education about sexual health have had some success.

Despite the enormous increase in reported sex crimes as well as more arrests and convictions, experts estimate that only one out of every ten sex offenders ever faces arrest. Perhaps something can be done in your community to address deviant sexual behavior, intervene in the lives of people who may act on their distorted desires, and stop sex crimes before they start.

- Call The Safer Society for information about programs nationwide that offer victim awareness training as well as offender prevention. Call 802-247-3132 or write:

The Safer Society Program & Press
P.O. Box 340
Brandon, Vermont 05733

- Consider some suggestions from a man imprisoned in Kansas for rape. He focuses primarily on ways churches could address sexual problems more directly.

Churches need to teach sex education . . . to the adults. Churches and ministers are deathly afraid to touch the subject of sexual relationships in light of Christian thought and behavior, (while) marriages and individuals are falling apart. Parents need to teach this information to their children. . . . This will assure the children that they can come back and ask bigger questions later, because the parents are on their side.

More open honesty needs to take place among men about their sexuality. . . . (Male church leaders) need to challenge and confess faults "one to another," setting an example to all men. Secrecy is the most powerful gasoline available to continue running a sexual offender's generator. Bring into these seminars men who are willing to confess and honestly admit sexual problems: perverse actions or fan-

tasies; use of pornography and its damaging effects; immoral behaviors and relationships. Then they could tell how they were lifted out of the mire. . .through confession/confrontation, repentance, counseling, accountability, etc.

Encourage men (who struggle with sexual difficulties) to get professional counseling.

Peter V., Kansas

"Most sex offenders against children were themselves victims of abuse when they were children. When they were child victims, we loved them, cared about them and professed a desire to help them. When they grew up and lived out the distorted desires they learned as children, we hated them and sought to cast them out. They merely grew older" (Todd R. Clear, Ph.D. From a speech delivered to the American Probation and Parole Association, 1992).

37. PUT YOUR FAITH TO WORK

People of faith are involved in changing lives in all sorts of ways which ultimately help prevent crime. Among Prison Fellowship volunteers, the basis for all ministry activity is the gospel of Jesus Christ. PF founder Chuck Colson sums up the organization's operating philosophy: "I would never be so presumptuous to say that only the gospel of Christ can bring about moral reformation. I'm happy about every effort where individuals help individuals. But it is Jesus Christ who made a lasting difference in my life. And this is what I can offer to others."

- **Pray.** Seek God's healing for victims of crime, families of prisoners, and prisoners themselves. Study God's word, the Bible, for insight concerning justice and how it may be achieved.

- **Share** what you are learning about the spiritual issues involved in crime prevention. Tell your pastor or small group or church lay leaders. See if there is an avenue through which your church may become more involved in the issue—perhaps through an outreach committee or local missions.

- **Ask** if there are ways you could share Christ with people whose lives have been wounded by crime. There is always a need for spiritually mature

Christians to lead Bible studies in prisons or to meet and pray with the spouses of prisoners.

- Become a member of Prison Fellowship's Intercessory Prayer Team. Join hundreds nationwide who bring to the Lord the needs of prisoners, families, volunteers, and prison ministry leaders. Call 1-703-478-0100.

- Do religious activities really make a difference among hardened prisoners? "Jailhouse conversions" are frequently characterized as being short-lived and meaningless once a prisoner gains release. Clearly not every profession of faith inside or outside prison is genuine. Yet Prison Fellowship and many other ministries to prisoners, as well as chaplaincy programs at most institutions, see another side to the story. Quiet and persistent efforts to meet with inmates for prayer, Bible study, and conversation engender a response from incarcerated people who, perhaps for the first time in their lives, have run up against an insistent need to search for answers and significance.

In 1992, PF brought more than 125 Christian recording artists, athletes, and speakers to 92 North Carolina prisons in an event called "Starting Line." Usually about 15 percent of the state's prisoners participate in religious programs, but Starting Line drew capacity crowds to prison gyms, cafeterias, and yards. Some facilities reported 90 percent participation.

To help with Starting Line, PF recruited 300 churches and 4000 volunteers to take part in a systematic, statewide plan to minister to prisoners, ex-prisoners, and their families. When it was over, an independent organization, the Center for Social Research, evaluated it and found a strong positive response across the board. One prison superintendent said, "Starting Line was a breath of fresh air which swept through the prison. The staff felt the inmates were engaged, liked the entertainers, were impressed by the sincere witness of some of the big name sport stars, (and) enjoyed listening to Chuck Colson speak." Another pointed out, "The presence of enough trained volunteers to reach the inmates one on one, the time allowed inmates to participate, the low-key presentation of the gospel, and the music all seemed to create a sense of purpose and community within the prisons."

Among prison superintendents, 83 percent said Starting Line increased inmate morale. More than 60 percent reported a positive effect on interactions among inmates and between inmates and staff; and 80 percent noted that the event made an impact on prisoners' religious values.

The events held in 1992 were just the beginning. Volunteers trained for the long haul have returned to those North Carolina prisons regularly to conduct follow-up seminars, Bible studies, and one-to-one mentoring. Whether prison ministry happens on a large scale, as it did here, or on a far smaller scale, it renews the hope of imprisoned people left too often in despair.

> *I wouldn't go as far as to say that Christianity is the only way to overcome defects of character, but it is the most productive aspect in life that I've seen and personally experienced.*
>
> Bob H., Indiana

38. BE A PARTNER AGAINST CRIME

Juveniles who get caught for the first time generally do not go to jail; they are placed on probation. It's at this point that young men and women are most readily influenced to change their criminal behaviors and destructive attitudes.

Yet the criminal justice system is frequently so overloaded that paid probation officers spend little time individually with the hundreds they are assigned to monitor. In Michigan, a group called Volunteers in Prevention, Probation & Prisons, Inc. (VIP) offers a creative solution to a worsening problem.

VIP designed a national program model, "Partners Against Crime," to link volunteers with young people on probation. Trained volunteers from all walks of life make a commitment to spend time individually each week with their assigned probationers. They are available to respond during times of crisis, to offer moral support, and to provide one-to-one attention that can keep these offenders from drifting toward a life of repeat crime.

- Find out if your community has a VIP program already in place. If not, VIP can send you their model program materials. Contact VIP National Program Headquarters, 163 Madison, Suite 120, Detroit, Michigan 48226. Telephone 313-964-1110 or fax 313-964-1145.

- Volunteers also serve as partners against crime by helping with program administration and management, gathering information about juveniles as they enter the system, or recruiting, screening, and supervising new one-to-one volunteers.

- The program is effective. In some cases, courts using the program have reduced recidivism by 50 percent. A study conducted by the University of South Florida at St. Petersburg found "The citizen-counseled group were employed more regularly, made greater educational progress, and appeared to be more responsible, less impulsive, and less rebellious than the group on regular probation." Frank E. Moody, director of administration for VIP and Partners Against Crime, adds:

"Volunteers bring two elements to the system that are not otherwise available: first, they have time to deal with the individual as a person and not as a file to be processed and moved out. This time translates into truly understanding what caused the problem and what is an effective and appropriate response to the criminal activity. Second, they are there because they care and have compassion for the offender and for the victims of crime. The element of caring is what changes lives and creates the relationships that are frequently absent from the lives of the offenders.

"The combination of time and compassionate, caring interest changes lives. No longer do we provide ten minutes a month from a probation officer, but hours of dedicated one-to-one time to help offenders work through a difficult time in their lives and reach responsible conclusions.

"The use of volunteers in criminal justice programs is only limited by the imagination of the courts and the volunteers. Programs have reported use of volunteers in pre-sentence investigations, in intensively supervised probation programs, and in every facet of the criminal justice system.

"Some common-sense precautions are needed for the use of volunteers. These include, but are not limited to:

- Don't place yourself in a situation in which you feel uncomfortable. Meet in public places, such as fast-food restaurants, libraries, and churches. Never go to the client's home or invite him or her to your home.

- Never give the client anything. Many clients in the justice system are experienced manipulators and will continue to take whatever they can get if they feel they can 'work' the volunteer.

- Friendships develop between the client and the volunteer, and friendship is the basis for making changes in a person's life. Friendships are based on trust, respect, confidentiality, and communication. Volunteers should do whatever is necessary to further the development of this friendship factor which will provide them the opportunity, eventually, to help the client through hard trials and choices in life."

39. BEFRIEND A PRISONER

Because so many prisoners get released and then rearrested, helping change a prisoner's life can pay big dividends for your community. Effecting change in the life of a hardened convict poses many more challenges than working with younger offenders just experimenting with crime. Yet changes are occurring even in the bleakest prison environments. Befriending a prisoner doesn't necessarily mean driving long distances or even going behind bars.

- Be a prisoner's pen-pal. Thousands of convicts want the encouragement that comes from regular correspondence. You can be matched with a prisoner through Mail Call, a program run by Prison Fellowship. Call 1-800-787-5245.

- Help a spouse find support. More than 90 percent of people in prison are men, and those who have wives experience severe marital strain. The wives frequently feel deserted, isolated, and misunderstood. They need to know someone cares. And they can benefit tremendously by meeting with others whose spouses are locked up.

  Prison Fellowship has helped individuals organize Spouse Fellowship groups in some 60 communities. Typically, the women meet in a volunteer's home for honest discussions about their circumstances and their feelings. They share a Bible study and prayer time and contact one another between meetings.

- Give a prisoner's kid a gift from Dad or Mom. Each year at Christmastime, churches throughout the country display trees decorated with paper angels. On each angel is the name of one prisoner's child. Churchgoers select a name and purchase a gift for that child. When it is delivered, the volunteers tell the child the gift comes on behalf of an imprisoned parent. More than 350,000 children received such gifts in 1993. One of them wrote a note saying, "Would you please tell my daddy that I said thank you for the presents and that I'm not mad at him anymore?" Volunteers from more than 10,000 U.S. churches help organize Angel Tree each year.

What difference does it make if you befriend a prisoner? A woman incarcerated in North Carolina writes,

When I came to (prison) I felt really bad about myself. Then I went to a (PF) seminar and started meeting volunteers. I was like a Chihuahua—really scared, and I shook all the time.

The volunteers were so loving and caring. They didn't care what I was in for. They love God, and they love me. It made me feel good about myself to know that people who didn't even know me took such an interest in me.

In 1991 I was picked to help rebuild a house for an elderly couple (through a PF Community Service Project). In 1992 I was picked again. It really encouraged me to make something of myself. I'm no longer the same person I used to be (Jubilee, January 1993, 3).

40. HIRE AN EX-PRISONER

Chuck Hughes, president of American Office furniture distributors, had a major project. He needed a reliable supply of workers who could learn to disassemble, transport, and reassemble modular office furniture. The turnover rate among his current laborers was too high.

Together with Prison Fellowship president Tom Pratt and businessman Maurice Weir, Hughes devised a plan to work with the District of Columbia Department of Corrections to employ D.C. prisoners and ex-prisoners. The project was a great success. Hughes met all his project deadlines. The client was pleased with the job. And turnover was low. One former prisoner, the work crew supervisor for this project, was later hired full-time by American Office.

- Nearly one-half of prison inmates were not employed full-time when they were arrested. Almost 40 percent were making less than $5,000 per year. And, partly because there is little vocational training, many inmates leave prison unprepared to compete for jobs.

- Don't turn down applicants just because they have served a prison term. If they have references and are qualified or trainable, give them a chance to prove they can make it.

- Let your local probation office know that you would consider hiring a probationer. Many probation programs and prerelease centers place their wards with local businesses. Your local Prison Fellowship office also may know of capable ex-prisoners looking for work.

- Through the Federal Bonding Program, financed by the U.S. Department of Labor, you may obtain insurance coverage to protect against employee theft or dishonesty for probationers, parolees, and others who are not eligible for commercial fidelity bond coverage. Contact any State Employment Service local office or call 1-800-233-2258 for information. Fidelity bonding offered through the federal program is free of charge for up to one year and does not have a deductible.

- Consider ways your business could train ex-prisoners. By giving them work, you may help an ex-offender support family members, pay restitution to a victim, and escape idleness that may lead back to crime.

- There are risks involved in hiring ex-convicts. Over the years, PF has found it is unrealistic to expect people with ingrained criminal habits to adjust naturally to a work environment after being institutionalized for a long time. To provide the special assistance these new hires may need, PF developed guidelines that call for us to evaluate the crime to make certain it is not incompatible with the position, to include one ex-prisoner in the interview, to conduct quarterly reviews of the employee's work, and to assign the ex-convict a mentor who meets with him or her weekly and holds the new hire accountable.

As a relatively middle-aged black man, with an education and a criminal history, jobs are hard to come by. I believe (state probation and parole boards) could assist those like myself from getting involved in criminal activities by setting up some sort of job bank. After all, while incarcerated we get used to putting in 6 to 8 hours a day for very small wages, where we also learn the fine art of budgeting on an income of $50 a month maximum. If we can earn that amount doing labor just think how appreciative we could be earning 5 times $50 a week. But until society realizes that we are still real people and start showing concern for the ex-con by giving him/her a chance, the crimes will continue to rise.

Fred P., Pennsylvania

CHANGING THE SYSTEM

As a young impressionable man I'm sent to prison to curb my criminal behavior. Prison—where violence and drugs are an everyday occurrence. Prison—where men speak of all the money, women and drugs they've had from stealing. I believe prison is the only answer for some men. But I believe that non-violent first offenders should be given a chance before being thrown into prison. What happens when you put a domestic dog with wolves? He either gets killed or he becomes a wolf!

Chuck K., Oklahoma

41. ASK HARD QUESTIONS

Stopping crime begins with knowledge and commitment. If you learn how to secure your home or keep your car safe and take the steps necessary to do so, you're much more likely to avoid crime. Similarly, if you understand what really goes on in the lives of prisoners and parolees, you will be able to vote more intelligently and perhaps advocate change that goes to the root of the problem.

Here are some questions you could ask about what's happening in your community.

1. *How much of my tax money is spent on building new prisons and keeping prisoners locked up?*

   Building a new prison in the United States costs an average of $85,000 per bed. It costs taxpayers an additional $17,000 to to $20,000 to keep one inmate in prison each year. And in many cases the prisoner's family is forced onto welfare. What are the figures for your state?

2. *How many prisoners are released back into my community each year, and how many are rearrested?*

   State and federal prisons operate at an average of 125 percent of their design capacity. They are so overcrowded that prisoners frequently gain release just so new convicts can be locked up (*BJS National Update*, July 1992). A study of 108,850 prisoners released in 1983 in 11 states found that 60 percent of violent offenders and 19 percent of nonviolent offenders were rearrested within three years. Their arrest charges included 50,000 new violent crimes after their release ("Recidivism of Prisoners Released in 1983," *BJS Special Report,* April 1989). How many return to your community?

3. *What services are available to help parolees find housing and work?*

Consider the plight of this parolee:

> *The state of New Jersey allows up to $100 to inmates when released from prison at the end of their sentence. With that $100, I first had to pay any unpaid fines owed. After paying my fines, I had $65 (with) which I was expected to find housing, food, clothes, and funds for transportation while looking for employment. It's needless to say I failed and turned to crime.*
>
> *I would have been more successful at my attempts if I had a complete list of agencies that are willing to aid people who have nothing upon release from prison. . . . Each employment agency in each state also publishes a list of programs they offer to everyone. (Seeing that list) would have helped me from returning, if only I knew all this the last time.*

Kirby P., New Jersey

In Maryland, the Montgomery County Pre-Release Center (PRC) provides a community residential alternative for offenders who are about to be released. It encourages and reinforces responsible behavior and legitimate lifestyles. At a minimum, PRC residents are released to the community with a job, cash savings and housing, as well as increased social problem-solving skills. The program has seen more than 6,400 participants go on to productive work and social adjustment. More than nine out of ten have not been reincarcerated during a two-and-a-half-year follow-up period, and complaints from the Center's neighborhood have been essentially non-existent (*Annual Report FY 1992,* Montgomery County Pre-Release Center).

42. CONSIDER WHAT IT MEANS TO "GET TOUGH" ON CRIME

What motivates our current response to crime and criminals, and why isn't it working more effectively?

Two ideas have led us where we are today: deterrence and rehabilitation. Deterring criminals means increasing the likelihood of conviction and the certainty of punishment. It may involve stiffening the prison sentence for a particular crime. The greater the punishment, the harder criminals will try to avoid wrong behavior, so the theory goes. Rehabilitating prisoners may mean placing them on probation so they can receive therapy or substance abuse treatment. In the prison environment, it means teaching life skills they can use after release to become productive, law-abiding citizens.

Each of these ideas has its merits. Yet neither one is accomplishing the goal of reducing crime. Partly, this is true because of the very nature of prison life. As one inmate explains,

> In prison, people are subtly taught that . . . they must be cold, capable of murder, demanding respect and glorifying a selfish attitude. . . . Whatever the solution to crime is, it sure isn't prison! At least not the way they are run in this country today. . . .
>
> I, and everyone I know who has been to prison, got worse and worse and worse. It was only by a chance

*encounter with the Lord Jesus Christ that my life changed,
and I'm not too sure yet just how changed it is.*

Adam Y., Virginia

Many who are involved in seeking criminal justice
reform, including Justice Fellowship (Prison Fellowship's
reform arm), advocate a different approach. Approximately half the people imprisoned each year are charged
with nonviolent crimes. These convicts need to be held
accountable, but appropriate sentencing for them might
not always mean a prison term. Where else can society put
them? If our national consensus about crime and punishment begins to change, then political choices to fund better
alternatives, such as work camps or community- based
treatment centers, might be taken more readily.

- Getting tough on crime means holding criminals
  personally responsible for their actions while preserving their dignity as individuals. In the tradition
  of "loving the sinner while hating the sin," efforts to
  punish and then welcome back the prisoner into
  society work best when the prisoner has support
  systems in place such as family, neighborhood, or
  employment. If a person gets thrown into prison,
  those ties will be severely strained if not severed.
  Preserving those ties by keeping a nondangerous
  convict out of prison greatly enhances the likelihood
  that he or she will shun future criminal activity.

- Getting tough on crime means honoring the rights
  of victims and their families. Meaningful accountability should be measured in terms of its impact on
  the prisoner's beliefs, thoughts, and actions, not by
  the yardstick of time served behind bars. Prisoners

whose sentences include restitution to their victims or face-to-face encounters with individuals they harmed often leads them to accept responsibility and to set out on a new path of reintegration back into society.

- Tough sentencing for nonviolent criminals may not include prison at all, or it may involve time behind bars along with other sanctions.

Words to ponder

"We must make some hard decisions about the criminal justice system. The present system cannot handle the volume of crimes, arrests, trials, and incarcerations that we are generating. We need shorter, simpler trials, definitive sentences that tell criminals exactly what their punishment will be, prisons that punish and deter, and treatment and follow-up that give ex-offenders incentives to leave the life of crime" (Roy A. Irving, Chief of Police, Rochester, New York).

Biblical basis

On what basis does Prison Fellowship promote a particular view of justice? PF was founded as an explicitly Christian organization. Our view of justice is rooted in the Bible, and the principles of justice we promote are, we believe, dimensions of God's character and demonstrated by his active intervention in human history.

The biblical view of justice involves relationships, reconciliation, and a restoration of peace (or "shalom") to a community. How does this apply to crime today? It recognizes that crime, first and foremost, involves one person hurting another. The "shalom" of the community is threatened and needs to be restored. Both the victim and the offender need to be reintegrated into the community, whenever that is possible.

A criminal justice system based on these values would restore the victim, hold the offender responsible, and promote reconciliation for both and for others around them.

43. SAY "YES" TO ALTERNATIVE SENTENCES

Many people hold an unrealistic view of the criminal justice system. They believe criminals either face harsh punishment by being locked up, or they "get off easy" by being placed on probation. In their book *Between Prison and Probation,* Norval Morris and Michael Tonry explain a variety of intermediate punishments that help keep nonviolent offenders out of prison while imposing meaningful punishments. Some of these include:

- **Intensive Probation.** Close monitoring by probation officers can make probation a real chance for change rather than a meaningless slap on the wrist. In Georgia, teams of two officers keep track of 25 probationers, enforcing curfews, making sure they report for work or community service, and seeing that they stick with treatment programs for drug, alcohol, or sexual abuse. The probationers pay a fee for the service, and the program's success rate is 84 percent.

- **Community Service Orders.** Placing a convicted offender in an unpaid position with a nonprofit or tax-supported organization to work a specified number of hours is a widely accepted alternative to prison. For nonviolent offenders, it is far preferable to short-term imprisonment which is extremely disruptive and expensive.

- **Fines.** Currently, fines are incurred for traffic offenses and other minor misdemeanors. Severely punitive fines, such as taking away an offender's home or car, have been viewed as unfair. Yet a prison term may exact an equally harsh financial toll while it degrades and dehumanizes the convict. Fines, backed by a reliable way to collect them, could impose financial calamity while permitting a convict to keep his job and stay with his family.

- **House Arrest.** The offender is required to be at home on evenings and weekends and at work or in treatment on weekdays. Sophisticated electronic monitoring devices permit officers to check on the offender.

- **Intermittent Sentencing.** Sometimes convicted persons will be sentenced to go to jail every weekend for a period of time. During the week, they remain free to live with their families and keep their jobs.

- **Restitution.** The offender must pay the victim for property loss or personal damages. Even though he remains free to go to work, the offender's pay is diverted into repayment, compensation to the state, family support, and savings to keep him from being drawn back into crime.

44. GO DIRECTLY TO JAIL

Filling leisure time, preparing for release, and maintaining family ties are among the most critical needs for prisoners. There are numerous ways members of the community can help make prison life more tolerable and model for prisoners a responsible approach to life.

- Take your expertise to prison. If you have particular skill in the arts, for example, you may find part-time or contract work teaching crafts, music, photography, drama, and other forms of self-expression. For information on where arts programs are most active, contact I-CAN, the International Correctional Arts Network, Delaware Dept. of Corrections, 80 Monrovia Ave., Smyrna, DE 19977.

- Discover a new labor force. Some people in business and industry have found inmate labor serves their needs and gives prisoners a head start when they hunt for work after release. Work programs such as manufacturing offer inmates a distinct advantage: they gain income, real-life work experience, and an employment record they can take with them.

- Forge a student connection. College students are in a unique position to relate to young inmates. In Florida, an English professor at the University of Miami developed "Meet the Author," a program in which university students go to the Dade County

Juvenile Justice Center School. There, they read and invite discussion on essays they have written.

The program costs nothing, and it works. Professor Joyce Speiller-Morris reports, "The youths are always clamoring for us to present more programs, and I have more students volunteering to participate than spaces to accommodate them."

- Make it easier for families to visit. On the grounds of Folsom Prison in California, a staff of volunteers runs Welcome House, a first stop for many family members on their way to visit a prisoner. Welcome House offers transportation, clothing which meets the prison's dress code, and child care so wives can spend time alone with their incarcerated husbands. Similar services are offered by the Matthew 25:36 House in Monroe, Washington, near the Washington State Reformatory.

(Adapted by permission from articles in *Corrections Today*, a publication of the American Correctional Association, August 1991.)

45. WATCH A COURTROOM PROCEEDING

If you've never been to court, chances are your view of the criminal justice system has been shaped by "Perry Mason" reruns or "L.A. Law." Yet courtroom realities often bear little resemblance to the high drama of entertainment media.

One way to learn how the criminal justice system works in your community is to visit a courtroom during a criminal proceeding. Observe how the defendant is treated, whether the victim is present or involved in the case, what the prosecutor and defense attorneys have to say, and how a particular judge passes sentence.

- How does it measure up with your view of justice? Is the dignity of individuals upheld or undermined? Is the outcome determined by technical details relating to the crime or by concern for restoring personal and public safety?

- Read news accounts of local arrests, trials, and sentencings. Are criminals who threaten your community—for instance, drunk drivers—treated consistently? Is public opinion making a difference in law enforcement efforts?

- When sentences are handed out, do they reflect a concern for both victim and offender? Are creative alternatives being put into practice, such as community service or probation with conditions for substance abuse treatment?

- Consider ways the system might be held account-able by citizens like you. Do you see something that ought to change? Let others know. Find out which groups are active in promoting changes in the system where you live. Link up with them.

If the system was more consistent in dealing with alcohol-related offenses, it would be taken more seriously. My two years' formal probation was revoked for a Public Intoxication which they aggravated and added to and that's how I ended up with three-and-a-half years total. . . . If all alcohol-related offenses were treated equally and justly, then a lot more of those "social drinkers" would think twice before getting behind the wheel to drive anywhere.

I was very lucky, in the sense that I never hurt nobody, out of the past four or five vehicles I totalled, but all it takes is one time to take a life. I thank God everyday that I was spared that tragedy.

Jim W., Indiana

My father is an ex-officer of the law in the city where I got in trouble (so) I was treated a lot different than most. The judge, a good friend of the family, dismissed nearly $2,500 worth of traffic violations with no effect on my license. The D.A. also a friend got my first felony dropped, never put on my record and just a slap on the wrist.

Those are only two instances of many where the law was bent to serve a friendship. I grew to learn that because of who my father was, I was immune to punishment. I wish that the first time I had ever been to court on a traffic viola-tion I would have gone to jail.

Bill T., Montana

46. SUPPORT TREATMENT FOR SUBSTANCE ABUSERS

I've been in trouble on several occasions, and on each occasion . . . I have requested a sentence of incarceration in the county's comprehensive drug rehabilitation program in exchange for a guilty plea. Unfortunately, Dade County's courts would much rather send people to prison. When I get to prison, I request to be sent to an institution that has a comprehensive treatment program, but unfortunately I am sent to institutions that are underdeveloped in that respect, and their main source of rehabilitation is putting a bush axe, pick, or shovel in your hand and saying, "Boy, get to work or you'll never get out of here."

Sooner or later, someone is going to have to realize that there are people begging for help, those who do not know how to help themselves.

Owen G., Florida

The war on drugs is changing, but the effect of policies put in place throughout the 1980s continues to permeate the criminal justice system at all levels. Consider the findings of Rand's Drug Policy Research Center: Between 1980 and 1992, the federal budget for drug control grew from $1.5 billion to nearly $13 billion, most of which funded enforcement programs. At the same time, penalties for drug offenses were dramatically stiffened. Mandatory sentencing fueled an increase in the number of people imprisoned on federal drug charges from 2,300 in 1980 to 13,000 in 1990.

Even so, illegal drugs remain widely available. Chronic drug use in the inner city feeds crime in three ways: drug-induced changes in mood and thinking ability make some users more violence-prone; users turn to crime to get money to buy drugs; and violence occurs as an inescapable part of trafficking in drugs.

- If you support treatment instead of imprisonment for drug offenders, let your elected officials know. Public opinion can make a difference, and quality substance abuse treatment programs work. Yet today there is no effective public drug treatment system.

- Spread the word about effective treatment alternatives. One is a national model program in Alabama, where a $2.4 million federal grant enabled the state to convert a prison into a drug treatment center with 600 beds. Nearly 80 percent of inmates who enter Alabama prisons have a history of drug abuse. The ones selected for this program are treated according to the severity of their addiction. To keep patients from reverting to drug use, there is an extensive residential aftercare program. At a "weekend in recovery," recovering members of the community attend meetings and workshops along with the inmates. Monthly family drug treatment seminars involve inmate families in the process (Debbie Herbert, "Grant Enables Alabama to Convert Prison into Drug Treatment Center," *Corrections Today*, August 1991, 216).

With respect to crime prevention, what I feel is of grave and fundamental importance is that (we) recognize—as the

*medical community has for 25 years—that chemical depen-
dency is a disease and treat it accordingly. . . .*

*In my particular case, what would have prevented me
from committing the crime that netted me a 13-year prison
term is not having picked up (after two years of sobriety)
that first drink and the inevitable dozens thereafter.*

*Sure, you can teach a man how to upholster or repair
sewing machines, but if he is going to resume his use of
drugs (which as we all know may never have been inter-
rupted just because he went to the pen for awhile), upon his
release, how valuable will his skills be? He'll never know,
because more than likely he'll never have the opportunity to
find out.*

Henry M., California

47. SHUN MEDIA VIOLENCE

Watching TV and seeing people do robberies and the way it has been glamorized on TV made me think of doing it myself, and robbery is why I am incarcerated.

Marvin C., Alabama

Overwhelming evidence points to a connection between media violence and crime. At a meeting of the American Psychiatric Association, researchers linked television with as many as half the crimes committed in the United States. Two surveys of young male prisoners convicted of violent crimes show between 22 percent and 34 percent said they consciously imitated crime techniques learned from watching television (Brandon S. Centerwall, "Television and Violence: The scale of the problem and where to go from here," cited in *Journal of the American Medical Association*, June 10, 1992).

Meanwhile, violence on television continues to escalate.

• Write letters telling broadcast executives what you think about violent programming. Let your local cable company know which channels air offensive shows.

• Commend networks and cable channels which respond positively to pressure for less violence. Television can clean up its act. Because of a changing social consensus, there are fewer TV heroes today who smoke or drink. The same can hold true for violence.

- Pressure elected officials to support legislation requiring that new television sets contain built-in time-channel lock circuitry. A time-channel lock gives parents greater control over what their children watch. This approach has worked before: A law passed in 1990 mandates that television manufacturers include closed-captioning circuitry for the deaf.

- Write an article for your PTA newsletter or community newspaper to explain why TV viewing should be limited. Ask for information from the National Coalition on Television Violence, P.O. Box 2157, Champaign, IL 61825.

- Join others to boycott advertisers. If they feel the pinch of financial loss, advertisers will not buy television time on programs notorious for their violence.

- Encourage broadcasters to send better messages— ones that could help stem the tide of substance abuse, for example. One inmate explains his ideas for this sort of ad campaign:

Nobody, and I mean nobody, likes being made to look like a fool. Imagine a (television) commercial, the camera zooming in on a parking lot full of expensive cars and well-dressed couples getting out entering a club. Inside the club, a huge banner proclaims a drug dealers' party. Men and women alike have their glasses raised in toast.

"To the people who made all this possible—crack smokers and junkies." They swallow their drinks and start laughing.

Another could show a user buying drugs from a dealer. It starts to rain. The user asks for a ride and the dealer says no. The user pleads, begs, tells of the hundreds of dollars he's spent with the dealer that day. The dealer tells him, "Look, I just sell you the stuff, I could care less if you live or die."

I'm not saying (these ideas) will end drug usage, but it will be part of the plan to curb it. Throw all the drug messages at the people every so often 24 hours a day. Don't let up. Hammer it home. Sooner or later, people will wake up.

George P., Texas

48. TAKE A STAND ON GUN CONTROL

"My own political disposition is conservative, but I'm not one of those who resists gun control and gun registration. I think it's going to become indispensable in America" (Charles W. Colson, National Press Club speech, March 11, 1993).

Astounding numbers of firearms—as many as 50 million—now circulate in the United States. Rarely do they stay put; guns are regularly stolen and resold. Handguns account for as many as 1,400 accidental deaths each year and tens of thousands of intentional woundings and murders. The federal government's National Center for Health Statistics reports that firearms cause more deaths among Americans ages 15 to 24 than all natural causes combined. Deaths by firearms for this age group are second only to deaths by motor vehicle accident.

If the demand for guns appears insatiable, the supply is virtually uncontrolled. Obtaining a license to sell guns is as simple as filling out a two-page form and paying $30. The U.S. Bureau of Alcohol, Tobacco and Firearms issued more than 270 new and renewed licenses each day in 1991—91,000 in all. Only 37 new applications were denied. Yet hundreds of federally licensed dealers have been taken into custody for criminal charges (Pierre Thomas, "Hit-or-Miss Control of Firearm Sales," *Washington Post*, 29 Nov. 1992, 1).

- Organize a weapon turn-in day. In May, 1993, more than 300 firearms were turned in to police officers in Washington, D.C., and its Maryland and Virginia suburbs. The program was modeled after a collection organized by a mother, Julie Elseroad of Ashton, Maryland, who became alarmed after a .357 magnum was found at her son's school. Fourteen churches served as collection sites. The weapons, which were accepted without any questions being asked, were destroyed after police checked to see if any of them were reported stolen.

- Write for information from the National Coalition to Ban Handguns, 100 Maryland Avenue, N.E., Washington, D.C. 20002. Another resource: Handgun Control, Inc., 1225 Eye Street, N.W., Washington D.C. 20005.

- Tell your elected officials what you think should be done to reduce the nation's proliferation of firearms. See that they follow through on promises to "do something" about the escalating gun violence.

I purchased the gun I used legally, and if there had been a nationwide check to see if I was a convicted felon (and I was), then I would never have gotten the pistol I used. There should be tighter restrictions on the sale of pistols.

Mel S., Illinois

(One day) when I was stoned out of my mind I went to a store, and in ten minutes' time I had a pistol and ammunition with only a driver's license. I phoned the police and told them my intent was to have a shoot-out with the police. Thanks to a few special cops who had befriended my mother

and brothers—they were on the scene, they knew of me and decided not to shoot or kill me if it could be helped. Thanks to those men and the almighty grace of God, my life was spared without incident. I received a ten-year prison term and spent three and a half years of that ten trying to get my life back together.

The Oklahoma law in regard to the process of buying a weapon should be revised. I believe it is too simple to get a firearm in our state. If there would have been the slightest waiting period, my life, I believe, would be much different.

William R., Oklahoma

49. BECOME AN ADVOCATE

As you consider crime prevention, think beyond your own home, family, and neighborhood. Consider ways in which changed lives and a changed criminal justice system could add up to real "get tough" policies against crime.

If you want to pursue goals beyond personal safety and security, you don't have to do it alone. Find out about others who already are working hard to stop crime. Here are some ideas to get you started:

American Association of Retired Persons (AARP), 1909 K Street, N.W., Washington, D.C. 20049. Call 202-434-2222.

Association for Victim-Offender Reconciliation, PACT Institute of Justice, 254 S. Morgan Blvd., Valparaiso, IN 46383. 219-462-1127.

Big Brothers/Big Sisters of America, 230 N. Thirteenth Street, Philadelphia, PA 19107-1510. 215-567-7000.

The Bureau for At-Risk Youth, 645 New York Ave., Huntington, NY 11743. 1-800-99-YOUTH.

Call for Action, 3400 Idaho Avenue, N.W., Suite 101, Washington, D.C. 20016.

Center for Conflict Studies and Peacemaking, Fresno Pacific College, 1717 S. Chestnut Ave., Fresno, CA 93702. 209-453-2064.

Citizens Against Crime, 1022 S. Greenville Avenue, Allen, Texas 75002. Call 1-800-466-5566 and ask for the phone number of your nearest regional office.

Citizens for Auto-theft Responsibility, Box 3131, Palm Beach, Florida 33480. 407-478-8990.

INFOLINK, 1-800-FYI-CALL

International Correctional Arts Network (I-CAN), Delaware Dept. of Corrections, 80 Monrovia Ave., Smyrna, DE 19977. 302-739-5601.

Justice Fellowship, P.O. Box 17500, Washington D.C. 20041-0500.

National Association for Christian Recovery, P.O. Box 11085, Whittier, CA 90603. 310-697-6201.

National Association of Town Watch, P.O. Box 303, Wynnewood, PA 19096. 215-649-7055.

National Clearinghouse for Alcohol and Drug Information, Box 2345, Rockville, MD 20847-2345. 301-468-2600.

National Crime Prevention Council, Information Services, 1700 K Street, N.W., Washington, D.C. 20006-3817. 202-466-6272.

National Fraud Information Center, a project of the National Consumers League, 815 15th Street, N.W. Suite 928-N, Washington, D.C. 20005. 1-800-876-7060.

National McGruff House Network, 1879 S. Main, Suite 180, Salt Lake City, UT 84115. 801-486-8768.

National Night Out, P.O. Box 303, Wynewood, PA 19096. 215-649-7055.

National Organization for Victim Assistance, 1757 Park Road, N.W., Washington, D.C. 20010. 202-232-6682.

National Victim Center, 309 West 7th Street, Suite 705, Fort Worth, TX 76102. 817-877-3355.

Neighbors Who Care, P.O. Box 17500, Washington, D. C. 20041. 703-904-7311

Parents Anonymous, 520 S. Lafayette Place, Suite 316, Los Angeles, CA 90057. 213-388-6685.

Prison Fellowship Ministries, P.O. Box 17500, Washington, D.C. 20041-0500.

Restorative Justice Ministries, 1717 S. Chestnut Ave., Fresno, CA 93702. 209-453-2064.

The Safer Society, P.O. Box 340, Brandon, Vermont 05733. 802-247-3132.

50. SPEAK UP

People who study trends in crime agree on one thing: as the year 2000 approaches, the problems posed by crime and a burdened criminal justice system are not going to vanish.

Even so, the news is not all bad. We hope this book has demonstrated that one person, one community, one program can make a significant difference. What may seem like a small effort may spark a following that spreads to other communities. Reading this book is just one way to find out how you can become involved in preventing crime.

The next step is up to you. Stopping crime will mean different activities for different people, but in almost every case, it begins when you get together with others and share knowledge and views on the issue.

So, speak up! Write a letter to the editor. Tell your neighbors. Recommend this book to others. And let us know what you've discovered and what you are doing. Prison Fellowship will send you information about our programs, publications, and addresses of our field offices nationwide. Write to us at:

Staying Safe Project
Prison Fellowship Ministries
P.O. Box 17500
Washington, D.C. 20041-0500